BULLY-PROOFING

BULLY-PROOFING

The Art of Social Confidence for Children

All power to the shields!

Steve Heron

Rev. date: 06/05/2013

To order additional copies of this book, contact:
Xlibris Corporation
1-800-618-969
www.Xlibris.com.au
Orders@Xlibris.com.au
503193

Contents

Dedicated to Skye and Milko

For Skye

I will continue to do what I can to make the world a better place.
Meoke will be free.

For Milko

Your words, *Will you leave me alone?* will always echo in my
memories.

Acknowledgements

I work mostly with primary-aged children. The majority of examples and stories I give come from my encounters and experiences with children on camps, in schools, in public, in families, and on holidays. I have a deep respect for each and every amazing child who has trusted me by talking about things that are dear to them. I hope I do them justice in this book, and by reading about their stories, I hope you will have a deeper respect for them and for all children.

I have changed the names of the children in the stories to protect their identity and privacy. I acknowledge their integrity, their spirit, and their patience with me and their journeys. There are too many to name. If you are one of these amazing people and you are reading this book, thank you.

I also thank the multitude of people I have worked with over the years as we have grappled with the issues surrounding social and emotional well-being of children and bringing about positive social change, so that the world will be a better and safer place for all children.

I appreciate the incredible work the staff in our school systems do, often under difficult circumstances and greatly underappreciated by the community. Teachers are a significant adult other than parents in children's lives. Often, teachers are called mum or dad by accident by children. This usually indicates a respect for the way teachers care for them.

Thanks to all the people who have listened to my thoughts, read my drafts, and allowed me to bounce ideas off them.

I would like to express my immense gratitude to the Nurture Works team and the St Mary's Community Care Board for believing in me, in the vision, and running with the crazy things that the BUZ initiatives have thrown at us over the last twelve years. Your support and sense of adventure is BUZtasmagorical.

I would like to make a special mention of YouthCARE (In Western Australia) who facilitate an incredible collective of chaplains, providing an underestimated, invaluable pastoral presence in public schools. For tens of thousands of children, their school chaplains are often their first point of contact when life gets tough. It is a pleasure to be associated with this dedicated and compassionate organisation.

A huge thanks to Sara Buxton from Sara Storm Photography for the awesome positive photo on the front cover and the great mug shot of me on the back of the book. Rikahn, Kara and Gabby, your smiles on the front cover are priceless, thanks.

It is a privilege to have Terry O'Connell write the foreword for my book. Thanks, Terry, I do use the Hoberman Expanding Sphere a lot, like you said I would.

Foreword

If you have ever uttered the word 'bully' then this is the book for you.

It is an interesting word that in today's society seems to dominate discussion when things are not going well at school or in our workplace. It always involves a range of negative emotions and would rarely be seen as a 'good news' story.

Well, things are about to change in that regard!

You will shortly learn that bullying is really about relationships and that those behaviours we tend to ascribe to the 'bully' are in fact manifestations of what happens when conflict occurs—conflict being a normal part of our day-to-day interactions with one another.

As soon as you begin to read this book, you are likely to feel yourself being drawn into the author's web. Through story, you will be taken on a journey. This story will become your own journey as you are challenged to make sense of something that most of us have taken for granted, 'everyone knows what bullying is!'

Eloquently, but simply written, the book contains a number of short chapters, each with a heading that reflects the main theme, and always built around a story. It will be your story or one that is well known to you. Be warned not to expect to be given solutions. You will notice that almost all the dialogue in this book involves questions of those seeking advice, and that without exception; all were able to work out what to do. The focus of each story is to reveal how relationships were harmed. These stories clearly illustrate why blame and punishment are not helpful.

Rather than suggest that this is a 'must read' for teachers and parents as a way of dealing with bullying behaviour, it has something to offer anyone who is interested in relationships. Don't be distracted by thinking this is for kids or about kids. Imagine being able to replicate the author's engagement style. Conflicts will never again be seen as a problem but as an opportunity for learning and personal growth.

Enjoy!

Terry O'Connell OAM
Australian Director, Real Justice

Introduction

It took some time to decide on the title for this book. I toyed with titles like

'Bullying; Myth, Media Hype, or Mega Issue.'
'How to Wipe Out Bullying.'
'Bully-proofing for Dummies.'
'The Truth Behind Bullying'

None seemed to be quite suitable. I finally settled on a title I am happy with:

Bully-Proofing—The Art of Social Confidence for Children (All Power to the Shields!)

I have used the word 'art' which suggests a level of skill or expertise. Bully-proofing is an art-form, and all children would benefit from the skills needed to build their social confidence which in turn will be one of their greatest assets.

At first, I didn't want the word 'Bully' in the title. This will become apparent when you read the chapters of the book. I bowed to the idea of including it in the title, mostly because I wanted to grab your attention. Even though it sounds negative, it is a starting point. Throughout the book, I will turn negatives to positives.

'Bully' or 'bullying' are emotive words. I decided to use the words and will carefully dispel any myths or misunderstandings about bullying so that we can call it for what it really is.

On some occasions, adults talk with me about bullying that they are currently experiencing. I tell them that the same principles I outline in this book are true for adults as well as children.

I purposefully don't quote many 'experts' or have extensive use of scientific research in this book. It is not my intention for it to be an academic work. I would much rather people of all walks of life find the book easy to read.

It is my intention to be somewhat controversial and challenging, but more so empowering.

I want my readers to feel challenged and encouraged. For some people, reading this book will revolutionise their thinking.

I have included many stories, some of my own childhood experiences. Sometimes I tell a story to help explain a point, sometimes I use a story to raise an issue, sometimes I just tell a story, like a work of art, I let you have your own interpretation. Sometimes you will relate well to particular stories, sometimes you might not. I have dispersed these stories throughout the book, most within the context of a chapter, but sometimes just for fun, I have placed a story in a random place. Enjoy!

Ultimately, I would like my readers to say, 'Now that is the most sensible stuff I have heard about bullying in my whole life.'

I am hoping that you find this book liberating.

I've set myself a challenge. I better deliver.

Chapter One

Childhood Memories of Bullying

The purpose of this opening chapter is to prise open some of the issues. I will tell you about some of the encounters from my own childhood. I'm hoping that in doing so, this will trigger in you some of your own memories; maybe memories of when you were bullied, or when you bullied someone else; maybe some painful memories.

Did I Get Bullied As a Child?

To be honest, I can't quite remember. I don't think I did. Does that mean it wasn't around when I was a child? Does that mean I was part of the problem? I don't even remember knowing the word 'bully' when I was a child. I don't have any specific memories of particular children bullying me, except maybe once in high school. I'll tell that story later in the book.

I know I didn't always get on with some children, and I didn't like some kids who thought they were tough. I do remember a girl who annoyed me when I was about eleven. She stole my eraser. She had the same initials as me 'SH'. When I went to claim my eraser back, she said it was hers. I was miffed, not bullied.

Milko

I'm ashamed of the way I treated some kids when I was a kid myself. I remember a boy at my primary school who was in the 'special class'. I don't remember his real name, but I do remember we used to call him 'Milko'.

Other than calling him that, I'm not sure how others or I were mean to him, but I do remember he used to lay on the ground writhing with his arms and legs in the air like an upside down cockroach trying to right itself. He would also call out, almost poetically, 'Will you leave me alone!'

I'm pretty sure I was part of the bullying culture around this boy. I wish I knew as much about respect then as I do now.

I wonder whatever became of him. It would be nice to come across him in some magical way after all these years and say sorry.

Rhonda

Another story I remember from my childhood days that still remains cemented on my memory.

I had a crush on a girl called Rhonda. I remember feeling awkward about having the crush and didn't know what to do. You know, that clumsy boyhood crush. One day, on the way home from school, I was walking behind her. She had a friend with her.

I wanted ever so much to walk with her and talk with her, but I didn't know how. I was as girl shy as you could get. So, I picked up a stone and threw it at the girls. It hit her friend smack on the noggin. Why did I do that? What was I thinking?

She and her friend didn't like me after that. No wonder! I had a bad reputation for a while amongst all the girls. I wonder if they saw me as a bully or just a silly boy. I think I was about ten. What happens to a boy's brain at that age?

New Friend

In high school, for a while, I hung around a group of guys that were a bit tough. Well, they thought they were. A new guy came to the school. Somehow I ended up being the one chosen to pick a fight with him. I don't remember voting on that.

I wasn't much of a fighter and didn't even know how to start a fight properly, but somehow I ended up having a go at him, with these supposed tough guys egging me on. I think the fight got interrupted because a teacher wandered in the vicinity. The tough guys cleared out and left the other guy and me standing there. I'm not exactly sure why I wasn't in trouble. The other boy had every opportunity to complain or 'dob' on me, but he didn't.

I can't remember exactly how it happened, but we became best friends from that moment. I no longer hang out with that group of guys probably because I didn't like the bullying culture they were caught up in.

School Reunion

When I hit forty, I went to a school reunion. The only one I have ever been to. It was fascinating catching up with a number of people that I went to primary school with. The first encounter was at the bar with a guy who had half of his thumb cut off by an axe accident (axe-ident). He showed me his thumb. Yep, a bit of it was still missing.

Another person I came across at the reunion was a guy who I remember being, as I recall, someone I didn't like. When I look back on it, I think I didn't like him because he just never treated me or anyone very well, and he was a smart A . . .

I remember asking him, 'So what do you do nowadays?'

To which he replied, 'What's it to you, are you a detective or something?'

I remember thinking, 'This is a school reunion. What sort of question did you think I was going to ask?'

He was a nasty piece as a kid in primary school, and it looks like he still was. He did go on to tell me though, that he had been married three times. In the back of my mind I was thinking, 'Doesn't surprise me.' A good friend of mine said, 'What goes round, comes around'.

What makes some kids so mean, so unlikable?

All of these encounters have something to do with bullying. It has been around since the year dot. Do I think it is any worse nowadays? I'm not sure. What do you think?

I'm thinking that it doesn't really matter whether it is better or worse.

I wonder what childhood experiences you thought of? Everyone has their own childhood bullying stories.

If we lived in a perfect world, people would be nice to each other all of the time, but we don't live in a perfect world, and children will encounter all kinds of relationship challenges. It would serve them well to be equipped with the skills to handle things when people don't treat them with respect. They would benefit from skills to handle things when being bullied rather than being just told to, 'Toughen up, princess.'

We will always encounter people who we don't like and who don't like us. We will see people being treated badly. We may even treat people badly ourselves. What matters is how we handle it and better still, how we can prevent it and how we can help our kids with these issues.

This is what this book is all about. Let's get stuck into it.

Chapter Two

What Bullying Is (And What It Isn't)

Everyone has the right to feel safe and be respected.

I conduct a large number of parent evenings on bully-proofing. After breaking the ice, I offer the statement, 'Everyone has the right to feel safe and be respected.' I check with everyone present that they agree. So far, no one has challenged the assumption or walked out on me.

With that as a starting point, I then ask, 'What is bullying? Or if you could give me a definition of bullying, what would it be?'

If I was to ask you the same question, I wonder what your answer would be.

The usual responses I get from the parents include, teasing, getting physical, hitting, excluding, not treating with respect, abusing, calling names, threatening, and so on.

I don't like many of the definitions I have looked up in various dictionaries. I imagine that I am the author of a world-class dictionary and present the audience with the following definition:

Bullying:

A repeated, persistent, or systematic action by one or more people that violates another's right to feel safe and be respected.

I used to say that bullying usually has a power imbalance, but over time, I have come to realise that bullying is *all* about power imbalance. I will elaborate on this throughout the book.

Let's talk about unhelpful ways of looking at bullying.

There are a number of *myths* surrounding bullying.

The first being this bad definition:

A bully is a bad person that picks on you.

A reputable charitable organisation used this definition in a television advertising campaign until they realised that it was outmoded and unhelpful.

For some reason, we label 'bullies' as bad people. Back in the 'good old days', one could have had an image of a bully as a big person, possibly someone who kicks sand in your face at the beach. You might conjure an image of the 'school bully', the one who steals kids' lunches, gives kids wedgies, grabs kids by the collar, or the like.

The image of the 'school bully' just doesn't cut it anymore.

At a recent talk I was giving, one of the parents was furious about a boy who had been picking on her son. She said that the boy was a bully and that he was evil and the devil incarnate. She said that something should be done to stop this boy from bullying others.

Later, in the evening, she was talking about her nephew who gets into lots of trouble at school, doesn't have any friends, and is often accused of bullying others. She went on to say that he is not a bad boy, that people just don't give him a chance, and that he just needs love. I found this interesting after what she had said about the other boy earlier in the evening. When I asked her to draw a comparison between the two boys, she was agape. 'Oh my goodness, they are the same! I was just looking at them in a different way.'

Ten Questions

I often play a game that I call 'Ten Questions' with children. I play this game just to get to know a child a little more, to strike up conversation, to find out about what children are thinking about and as a form of social research. I ask a child if I can ask them ten questions. The questions are random and varied. Some easy, like, 'What is your favourite colour?' 'What would you do if you found $50?' Some difficult, like, 'What's the saddest thing that has happened to you?' 'Who is someone that inspires you?'

I am always blown away by the kinds of answers I get. Sometimes children tell me some amazing things and some deep things. I often ask them after a difficult question if it is OK to continue. They always say yes. In fact, they often beg me to continue, almost as if they have been waiting for someone to ask these kinds of questions for a long time.

One of my favourite questions is 'If you were the principal of the school, what would you change or what would you make better?'

By far the most common answer I get is 'I would get rid of the bullies'.

This intrigues me. I want to find out more, so I often ask, 'Who are the bullies in the school?'

Most of the time, they don't actually know. It's almost like there are mythical bullies in the school, kind of like the boogie man. Sometimes children may name a child or two. Usually, they name children who have some behaviour management issues and may have outbursts of anger. My guess is that children feel a bit afraid of these children and possibly feel unsafe when they are around.

In a primary school, there are no 'bullies' per say, just some children who have not developed positive social and emotional skills.

Chapter Three

The School Bully?

A young fellow, I'll call him Tristan, ten years of age, came for a chat one day because he was having trouble with a boy who was threatening him. The boy who was threatening him was a child who had some behavioural issues. He had difficulty managing his anger and would often go into fits of rage, mostly involving a whole pile of expletives and abuse flowing from his mouth. This abuse was often aimed towards teachers.

Because of this, the boy had a reputation with the other students and also amongst the parent community. He was often labelled as a 'bully'.

Tristan came to get some advice on how to handle him. Tristan had been to see me before about some friendship issues, and some of his friends had come to see me about how to handle him. Tristan is a short, stocky fellow who is good at sport. He has an incredible amount of integrity and always wanting to do what is right. His mates said that he can be quite bossy. I saw leadership traits that needed some guidance and coaching.

Tristan and the other boy had rubbed up against each other. Most other children avoided the boy but Tristan stood up to him. This created a tension between the two boys, and Tristan was a bit worried because he knew the other boy could be quite aggressive.

I worked through the bully-proofing tactics with him, but there was an ongoing amount of tension. I suggested that we could do a restorative session with himself and the boy. He was very reluctant at first. I was a little suspicious as it appeared to me that Tristan himself had been doing a certain amount of the provoking and was possibly worried that he might get found out. I was a little nervous as I had not had any one on one with the other boy and wondered how it would go.

A couple of weeks passed, and I found out from the school admin that an out-of-school incident had happened that was reported back to the school by the mother. I offered to do the restorative session with the boys. The deputy spoke to the other boy, and I spoke to Tristan. They both agreed. The deputy came in on the meeting to see the process and offer support to us all.

The restorative practice process is incredibly powerful. I have never done a restorative session that doesn't have a positive outcome, but I was nervous. I won't go into the full process on this occasion; you can read more about it later in the book and in one of the chapters of my previous book *BUZology*.

I started by saying to the boys that I was aware that there was a problem between the two of them. I told them that I will do my best not to take sides and will listen to them both equally and give them both a chance to speak. More so, I told them that I will help them to really listen to each other. I asked them if they both agreed to talk about it and find a way to make things better. They both agreed. Phew!

I got them to face each other and tell each other what they think happened and how they felt about it. I got Tristan to go first. He said that the boy had been picking on him and that he felt upset and angry. He talked about the incident on the weekend when the boy walked past his house and abused him, his friend, his dad, and his friend's dad.

The other boy was amazingly self-controlled. He listened without being irrational. When it was his turn to speak, he said that he didn't like the way Tristan had been looking at him and giving him the finger. He also talked about the incident on the weekend. He said that the boy's father actually started the incident. He said that as he walked past the house, the father called him a 'pussy'. He said that the father had said that he's not so tough now that he is outnumbered.

The boy said that he tried to control himself and did leave, but it played on his mind. He came back and hurtled a whole pile of abuse back at the boys and dads.

This is when the boys and dads went inside and the mum found out about it. It was this that the mother reported to the school, that the boy had been bullying her son and had abused all of them at their house.

The boy was amazing. He stayed composed and spoke with honesty and integrity. He was upset and angry about what had happened. He believed that he had been provoked. I checked with Tristan what he was thinking about what the other boy said happened.

Tristan told me that it is exactly what had happened. He said that he felt 'bad' that his dad had started it, but he also felt strong because he had his dad, friend, and friend's dad there.

It's a tough life for kids who get a reputation and try to shake it. It seems that the whole world feels self-justified when we back these kinds of kids into the labelled corner that we think they should belong. If only we treated them with the respect that they also deserve, we can help them to turn their own lives around. We have to give them a chance. In this case, the parents were the provokers, and the boys were the pawns.

Tristan was ashamed at the way he had been behaving. He liked the power, but he was growing to not like himself. He actually said to the boy that he was sorry.

After asking them if they heard each other and how the other felt, I asked them both what they would like to happen now. Tristan said that he didn't want the boy to call him names anymore or bump into him to act tough. The boy said that he didn't want Tristan to try and act tough around him, especially when he had his mates there. He also said that he didn't want his dad to call him names anymore and to leave him alone.

The boys agreed on the request of each other. This isn't some magic fairy-tale outcome that took a simple conversation. It took over an hour. The deputy remained silent almost the whole time. I had to work hard to guide the conversation. The boys were incredibly cooperative and helpful. The deputy was amazed that what at first looked like one child 'the aggressor' being held accountable for his actions turning out to actually be the victim.

With Tristan's permission, I had a good conversation with his mother. She was surprised and annoyed with her husband. She was supportive of her son. They had a family meeting and discussed the issue.

I remember Tristan telling me once that his dad said to him to just hit the other kid. He told me that he didn't want to and that he was a better person than that. He was confused though because his dad and mum were giving him different advice.

On many occasions, I ask children what advice their parents give them, other than 'stay away from them'. The other advice that some parents give (mostly dads) is to hit them. I don't condone violence.

I ask these children, 'What do you think of that advice?'

They usually say that they don't like it because it is wrong.

I think what the parents are trying to communicate is for their child to stand up for themselves. That is a good thing, but there are better ways than hitting.

Tristan and the boy? There were no further incidents. I checked with them both, and they don't rub up against each other anymore. They seem to have a form of mutual respect. I've actually seen them playing together. I believe this was a turning point in the other boy's life. Since this encounter, I have heard more positive comments from school staff and other children about him than I have before. I'm not suggesting that this was the panacea, but one of the myriad of strategies that helped make the school a more respectful community and the boy to gain more respect and self-dignity.

I would also like to commend the deputy and her approach to the whole incident. Her support for both boys and their families was amazing. Her feedback to me was also rewarding.

A Little about Restorative Justice

I had heard about Restorative Justice or Restorative Practice and was presented with an opportunity to attend a conference where it was the keynote topic. Terry O'Connell was the presenter, and I was impressed with his presentation.

Restorative Justice is a philosophy, not a model, and ought to guide the way we act in all of our dealings. In his talks, Terry says that Restorative Justice is not just a tool that people can put in their toolboxes; it is the toolbox itself.

Restorative Justice finds its roots in the ancient traditions of the Maori and is incorporated into New Zealand's Law. It is an ongoing effort to reform our current criminal justice system. Restorative Justice is a way of seeing crime as more than breaking the law—it also causes harm to people, relationships, and the community. So a just response must address those harms as well. If they are willing, the best way to do this is for the parties themselves to meet to discuss the harms and how to bring about resolution. Sometimes those meetings lead to transformational changes in their lives.

Restorative Justice is about the 'offender' hearing how their actions have had an impact on the other. When they are aware of other people's feelings, they discover how victims and others have been affected by their behaviour, therefore allowing them a chance to have empathy for those affected.

When merely punished, a person can react defensively and therefore be distracted from noticing other people's feelings. With punishment, offenders are passive. In Restorative Justice, they are asked to speak. They face and listen to those whom their actions have affected and then help decide how to repair the harm.

A great book to read on Restorative Justice is, *Real Justice: How We Can Revolutionize Our Response to Wrongdoing*, by Ted Wachtel, The Piper's Press.

Restorative Justice is a relational approach that states:

> The stronger the relationship, the less likely we are to act inappropriately toward another.
>
> (Terry O'Connell)

I realised that I had been doing restorative justice all along. I was using a process that enabled children to restore relationships in a fair and respectful way. Doing some restorative justice training sharpened my skills and gave me a greater understanding of the importance of the process.

In Terry's words:

> We cannot be effective as practitioners unless we are able to integrate restorative justice principles and practice into our own lives and professional practices.

Chapter Four

There Is No Such Thing as a 'Bully'!

That's a bold thing for me to say!

Don't get me wrong—people do bullying things.

I believe it doesn't help to use the term 'bully' nor is it respectful, in the same way that it is not helpful or respectful to call a child 'bad'.

An upset mother came to see me because she received a letter from the school principal saying that her son was a bully. I asked her to tell me about it. I knew the school had a 'zero tolerance' to bullying, and I had read the school's bullying policy.

She said that by lunchtime, her son had been involved in three incidents that were considered bullying. Allegedly, he was physical with a group of ten-year-old boys. On the first occasion, he was warned by the duty teacher, in line with the school bullying policy. On the second occasion, his name was recorded, and on the third occasion, his name was submitted to the principal, who wrote to the parents saying that their child has been involved in bullying others and that the school has a zero tolerance to bullying.

She told me this as she sobbed and added, 'My son is not a bully! He is only five years old.' Her son was in pre-primary. It was his first day at school!

In no way do I condone his physical outburst with the other boys, but I seriously doubt that this was bullying, at least not according to my definition. The power imbalance? A group of ten-year-old boys and one five-year-old child, whose brain is wired for self-defence. This boy was not a bully and calling him one was not helpful. Who would like their child to have such a label from an early age?

The reality is that we all have the capacity to bully another, and we possibly have done it at some time. We don't go around labelling ourselves as bullies. We have all possibly stolen something in our life, that doesn't mean we get the label of 'thief'.

By the way, anyone who says that there is bullying in pre-primary probably has a wrong definition of bullying.

Chapter Five

Zero Tolerance

Over the last fifteen or so years, I have seen a number of approaches to reducing bullying in schools. The first being *zero tolerance*. While it is sensible to aim for zero tolerance with bullying, schools that ran with this policy had a tendency to err on the side punishing the bully. This policy meant a tendency towards authorities being informed of bullying, and consequently, the bully would get into trouble.

In one school, I saw on the library door a large poster that read, 'Dob in a Bully'. Not helpful! This policy tends to feed the triangulation of bully, victim, and rescuer.

The zero-tolerance policy often creates a policing and punitive approach, which serves to feed the triangulation.

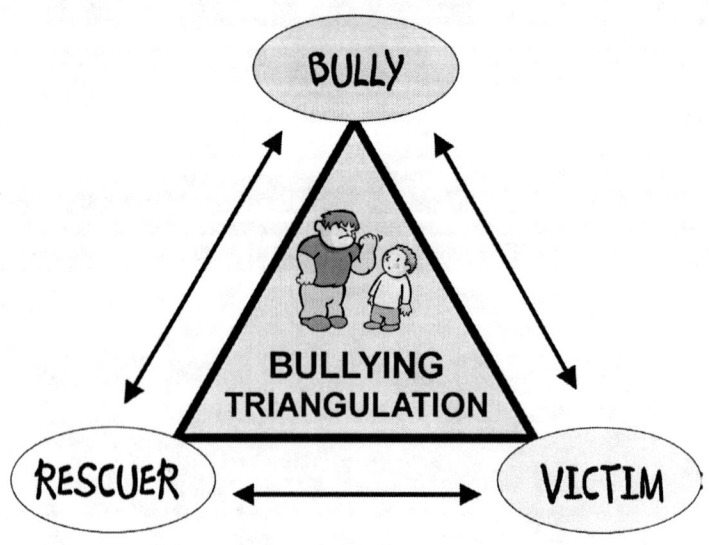

A simple explanation of this process:

One person (the bully) 'bullies' another (the victim). The victim then behaves 'victim-like'. They follow the school policy and let the authorities know (what schools call 'telling a teacher', and what kids know as 'dobbing').

The authorities respond to the incident, and the child who has not treated the other with respect is punished for bullying the other.

This punishment can come in many forms including, being told off, time out, suspension, forced to apologise, letter to parents, and so on. This child is now resentful towards the child that got them in trouble, and the bullying can escalate and often manifest in more subtle forms.

The 'victim' is not empowered. The 'rescuer' may actually act in a 'bullying' way to the 'bully'. They don't learn right from wrong, because they are only punished for doing wrong.

Thus the triangulation is complete.

A report issued by the American Psychological Association (APA) at their summer 2006 annual meeting found that zero-tolerance policies in use throughout US school districts have not been effective in reducing violence or promoting learning in school. The report called for a change in these policies and indicated a need for alternatives, including restorative practices such as restorative justice conferences.

The report was written by an APA task force, led by Cecil R. Reynolds, Ph.D., of Texas A&M University.

Chapter Six

Brendan, Bronwyn, and the School Bag

I would like to tell you this story because it brings to light the need to have creative, thoughtful ways of resolving bullying and conflict without a simple swipe of the punitive brush. It is a story that compares traditional punitive forms of handling aggression as opposed to restorative forms.

Brendan was a boy who had a reputation that was hard for him to shake, the kind where he was often the topic of discussion and the brunt of many jokes in the school staff room. Bronwyn was an acquaintance of his. I say acquaintance because no one really wanted to be his friend. The two at least had some kind of friendship.

Brendan was suspended for hitting Bronwyn with his school bag. As all the children did, when Brendan did something wrong, he got dobbed on. An incident happened between the two which led to Brendan being summoned to the office and confessing to hitting Bronwyn with his bag. There were no other questions except possibly that unhelpful, blaming question, 'Why?' To which Brendan probably just shrugged his shoulders. He was suspended for a day. A crime had been committed, a school rule (law) had been broken, and Brendan had to accept the consequences.

The day Brendan returned to school, both he and Bronwyn made separate approaches to talk with me. Brendan was first. He told me that he felt bad about what he had done, but he also told me that Bronwyn had been taunting and teasing him and he just got angry with her and swung his bag. The bag hit her on the head. Not his intention, but it happened.

It was in line up for a class. Bronwyn was hurt; she told the teacher what happened. Brendan felt that an injustice had been done. He had realised that what he did was not good, but he felt that the teasing he received from Bronwyn went unchecked. He still wanted to be friends with her, but he was still angry with her. Actually, he resented the punishment he received and had channelled his anger towards her. Supposedly, the punishment was meant to teach him right from wrong.

He told me that he didn't want to feel that way. I asked him, 'Did anyone ask you or Bronwyn to talk about this together?'

'No!'

'Were you offered a chance to say sorry to Bronwyn for what had happened?'

'No!'

'Have you spoken with her since?'

'No!'

'Would you like a chance to do that?'

'Yes!'

I told him that I would ask Bronwyn if she was OK about the idea of coming to talk together about what had happened and try to repair things. He was OK with that.

Bronwyn came to see me next. The first thing she said to me was that Brendan got suspended and that she felt bad about it.

I asked her what she meant. She said that she was teasing him about something and he got mad with her and hit her with his bag. She said that it hurt and she cried. The teacher saw her crying, so she told the teacher what had happened. We know what happened next.

She told me that she felt bad because he got suspended and that she didn't want to get him in trouble and that it was partly her fault.

I asked her, 'Did anyone ask you or Brendan to talk about this together?'

'No!'

'Were you offered a chance for Brendan to say sorry to you?'

'No!'

'Does Brendan know how you feel about it?' 'Have you spoken with him since?'

'No!'

'Would you like a chance to do that?'

'Yes!'

I told her that Brendan had already been to see me and wanted the opportunity to come to talk together about what had happened and try to repair things.

The two met with me. Bronwyn was the first to say sorry to Brendan for teasing him and getting him in trouble. As they looked at each other's eyes, I could see that there was clearly empathy that the two had not had a chance to experience since the incident. Brendan was apologetic. Their relationship was not only restored but strengthened as they communicated with each other in a safe environment, without interference from peers.

Kids don't ever have the chance to develop a full sense of empathy unless they are confronted in a respectful way with the outcomes of their actions and the effect of those outcomes on the other.

In this case, the two children were not initially presented with the opportunity to see how their actions affected the other, to listen to each other, to have empathy, to resolve their differences, and to restore their relationship. The punitive process used actually had the effect of driving a wedge between the two of them. After the punishment, there was no follow-up. The children were left to their own devices with strong feelings of guilt and resentment.

> Punishment is preoccupied with blame and pain. It does not consider the reasons for or look for solutions. It pre-empts more constructive ways of relating to a child. It drives people further apart, and it enables the parent and the child to avoid dealing with the underlying causes of the bullying. The overriding concerns of punishment are What rule was broken? Who did it? And What kind of punishment does the child deserve? Punishment deprives the child of the opportunity to understand the consequences of their actions, to fix what she has done, or to emphasise with the child she has harmed.

(Barbara Coloroso, *The Bully: The Bullied and the Bystander*)

Chapter Seven

The No Blame Approach

Another approach was called the NO BLAME approach. While not being entirely at the other end of the spectrum to zero tolerance, a culture of not blaming became prevalent. This often meant that a person who showed disrespect for another in a bullying fashion was not punished for their actions and on many occasions, not held accountable. This policy tends to create systems where children who feel bullied are not empowered and their parents feel that the school is doing nothing.

I sat in on a 'No Blame approach' session conducted by a principal with two children. Whilst the principal was fair and respectful to the two boys, because there was an emphasis to not blame either child, it seemed as if there were blinkers to what was really happening. The boy who was being picked on came away feeling disempowered as he believed that the actions of the other boy were ignored. The other boy felt like he got away with it which gave him a sense of more power. The bullying didn't stop.

While there is a little merit in both approaches, zero tolerance and no blame neither actually quite hit the mark.

It does not matter if it is mild, moderate, or severe: Bullying is not normal. It is anti-social and needs to be addressed as such. This is why current zero-tolerance policies (those that attempt to respond to a one-on-one fight, bullying, and assault with one solution—expulsion) are really zero-thinking policies. Such policies are about efficiency and finding fault, not about effective solutions for breaking the cycle of violence. What needs to be found is a social solution to this anti-social activity.

(Barbara Coloroso, *The Bully: The Bullied and the Bystander*)

Like Barbara's comments about zero tolerance being zero-thinking policies, zero-tolerance policies are as effective as cutting a birthday cake with a hammer.

No blame approaches hadn't been thought out well either. The sentiments were warm and fuzzy, as effective as cutting a piece of steak with a feather.

When someone has wronged another person, when lack of respect has been shown, when bullying has occurred, there needs to be accountability, without the damaging accusations of blame. Barbara is right! True bullying is anti-social, but could it be that punitive forms of righting these wrongs or lack of action may also be classed as anti-social?

Chapter Eight

Why Punishment Doesn't Serve Us Well, Why Kids Bully and Chocoholism?

It is a wrong assumption that people who bully others should be punished.

There is a belief in our society that we should respond to wrongdoing with punishment. This usually operates under the false expectation that punishment causes children to learn right from wrong. Punishment doesn't serve us well. Some researchers suggest that punishment is a very ineffective process of teaching right from wrong.

If bullying is about power imbalance, then responding to bullying with punishment is then responding to bullying with another form of bullying, because after all, punishment is about power.

I am not saying that people who do not respect another person's right to feel safe and be respected should not be held accountable, on the contrary. With the way that punishment is dispensed, the person who has bullied another is often not held accountable in an acceptable or contrite way. Often, the child who is punished becomes more resentful and vindictive.

Piggyback Fight and the Ripped Pocket (or My Broken Pride)

It's amazing what you can remember from your childhood. I am convinced, and I have read some research that says that people remember moments of strong emotion or strong sense of injustice from their childhood. This is certainly the case in my next childhood story.

When I was in about year six at primary school, a whole pile of other boys and I were involved in the biggest and the best piggyback fight I have ever been in. None have rivalled it since. I think it was against the school rules, but boys will be boys. I remember I had a great mount. I think his name was Allan. He was the best. I wasn't a big guy. He was. He was a gentle giant. We made a ferocious team.

Somehow the pocket of my regulation grey school shirt got ripped almost totally off. I remember wanting to get revenge or something like that. It was in the heat of the moment. I knew I was going to get busted when I got home, so I supposed in my illogical eleven-year-old brain that to rip someone else's pocket would give me some peace of mind or retribution.

I did it. I ripped some other kid's pocket, just as a teacher happened on the scene.

Out of the multitudes of kids involved in the battle, Allan and I ended up in the office. We got the cane. I think the head master said something nonsensically brilliant like, 'We have to make an example of you boys for the others.' Not sure what it meant. The cane hurt, but nowhere near as much as my pride and the sense of injustice of it all.

Did I learn the error of my ways? Did I learn right from wrong? I already knew what was right and wrong. No piece of thin wood across my hand was going to make any difference to my morality except to possibly introduce me to the concept of resentment. I didn't learn to respect authority that day. I learnt to be suspicious of it, fear it a bit, but also learnt this particular authority didn't seem to care about fairness.

My pocket was ripped. Not the first time. My pride was hurt. Not the first time. I did something bad. Not the first or last time. Did I feel sorry about ripping the other kid's pocket? Hell, yeah. I knew it was wrong and took some time to forgive myself. Looking back on it now, I wish I was given the opportunity to talk with the other boy about it. That's just the way things used to be.

Schools are the breeding grounds for our society's negative subcultures. Schools do not intend to hurt children, but like much of the rest of our society they often respond to wrongdoing with punishment. They operate under the false expectation that punishment causes children to change their ways.

We have all grown up in a punitive system and have rarely questioned it. Like our politicians, school administrators keep trying to satisfy a concerned public by being tougher and punishing more severely.

(Ted Wachtel, *Real Justice: How We Can Revolutionize Our Responses to Wrongdoing*)

Why Do We Still Have Bullying in Schools Today?

It was Abraham Maslow who said, *If the only tool you have is a hammer, you tend to see every problem as a nail.*

When things continue to go wrong, we often try to fix things with increasing amounts of the same ineffective solutions.

I remember visiting a school on their assembly day. It appeared that there had been an increase in bullying in the school of late. The principal stood up in front of the entire school community and said, 'There is a lot of bullying going on in the school and it has got to stop.'

That was it. That was his creative approach to anti-bullying in school. It reminded me of the times my brothers, sister, and I were in the back seat of the car, bickering and fighting.

My dad would call out from the driver's seat, 'If you kids don't stop fighting, I'm going to stop this car.' However, we would keep fighting. He would stop the car. We would stop fighting for a while, at least the physical part. It was never a permanent solution.

Izzy Kalman says that there are reasons for the limited success of anti-bullying programs that have been tried in our schools.

1. When experts tell students how terrible it is to tease and bully other kids and that these behaviours shouldn't be tolerated, it may get some kids to be more considerate towards others. However, this message is a double edged sword. It also gives students the message that they should get upset when they are on the receiving end of teasing and bullying. Thus, when they are picked on, instead of shrugging it off—which is the smart thing to do, they are more likely to think, 'How dare they treat me that way!' Getting upset by bullying has the unintended effect of perpetuating bullying.

2. Students are being instructed that 'telling is not tattling.' They are being encouraged, and in some schools even forced, to tell whenever anyone bothers them or when they witness others being picked on. Informing the authorities on people is about the best legal way to get them to hate you and to want revenge against you. It you are not sure of this, try this simple experiment: The next time your neighbours do something you don't like, call the police on them.

3. School personnel are being required to intervene when kids quarrel. Unfortunately, this almost always escalates hostilities. In fact, most of the bickering and fighting that goes on between kids is actually caused unwittingly by the attempts of adults to make kids get along. Thus, educators are being required to do the very thing that makes kids fight.

(Izzy Kalman, Bullies to Buddies: How to Turn
Your Enemies to Friends)

Izzy is pretty provocative. He basically suggests most of what schools have been doing is actually making it worse. I agree. If we really want to see a change, we need to find more effective, respectful, and sensible approaches, approaches that encourage positive relationships, restorative practices, and community building.

Why do children bully others?

I don't wish to spend a lot of time on this or speculate too much. When I ask children why kids bully others, they say things as follows:

'They are just trying to be cool.'
'They get treated like that at home.'
'Because they are just mean.'
'They don't like me.'
'They have an anger management problem.'
'They have something wrong with them.'

That pretty much sums up what children think. Why do you think children bully others?

When I ask children who others consider to have bullying behaviours the same question, they give me the same kinds of answers. However, when I ask them if *they* have ever bullied anyone, they tell me that they haven't. Hmmm. A lot of the time they may not be aware that they have bullying behaviours. They are just trying to defend themselves and stand up for themselves.

We are animals after all. The drive to survive is embedded in children's DNA. Part of this survival is the need to protect oneself. You may have heard of 'fight' or 'flight'. Depending on the level of threat, the circumstances surrounding the threat and their own skills will affect their own response.

Often, children are in conflict with each other as they compete for things: belongings, attention, friends, acceptance, and popularity. These things are at the core of social survival for children. When children come into conflict with each other, they employ the fight or flight response. Sometimes, this means they don't treat the other child with respect. Sometimes one gets the upper hand. Remember that bullying is all about power imbalance. The child who uses fight tends to overpower the child who uses flight. Hence, the power imbalance, which is interpreted as bullying.

Where my chocoholism started?

I have this theory as to one of the reasons why some children continue to bully others.

When I was twelve years old, I discovered the precarious world of shoplifting. I stole a bar of chocolate from a supermarket. I was smart, so I thought. I had a small amount of loose change. I went into the supermarket and chose something to buy with my small amount of money. I then went to the confectionery isle and thrust a bar of chocolate into my shorts. I went to the checkout and nervously paid for my small item. I knew what I was doing was wrong, but still did it. Phew, I got away with it.

I tried it again some days later, a little less nervous this time. I got away with it again.

I tried it the third time. As I brazenly strolled up to the checkout, I was asked by the woman who was serving me to remove the chocolate from my shorts. My heart jumped up into my throat. I had been sprung! I still remember the feelings as if it happened yesterday.

As I said, I knew it was wrong, but I kept on doing it. I took a risk, but because I got away with it, I became complacent. I felt terrible, guilty, ashamed, fearful, and remorseful.

The woman asked me for my name and address and said that my parents would be informed and that my name would be handed to the police.

I was thinking, 'If my parents find out, I am dead meat.'

When I look back on it, I am so glad I got caught. Because I knew it was wrong, I needed a jolt, a reminder of what my own morals were.

It wasn't forthcoming from that part of my brain that handles stuff like that, because the addictive nature of chocolate and the thrill of not being caught were too strong.

I was more devastated by the thought of letting myself down than I was of getting punished.

What was I going to say to my mum? What would she say to me? As it was, she never spoke to me about it. To this day, I'm not sure if she ever found out or whether she knew all along but just let me work it out for myself. Mums can be clever like that.

I know that I have never stolen anything since. I don't even buy cheap copies of DVDs in Asian countries because I believe it is a form of stealing. I might have stolen a pen from a workplace once.

It wasn't the fear of punishment that corrected my morality and put me back on the straight; it was being confronted with the truth about something I knew was wrong. I cemented my own values in spite of not being punished.

The connection with why children may continue to bully others.

I believe that most children who get caught up in the power of bullying (not treating others with respect on a recurring basis) know it is wrong. They continue to do it, partly because they get some power out of it. It's not because they haven't been caught, but because they haven't been confronted about it in a respectful, challenging way; a way that enables them to reflect on their own morals and challenge themselves to stick by them.

Like in my shoplifting experience, children need a moral jolt from time to time so they can pull themselves up and do what they know is right.

How do we stop children from bullying? How do we confront children in a respectful way? How do we help balance the power? How do we get children to take responsibility for their actions and improve relationships? How do we bully-proof children?

In the remaining chapters, I will endeavour to enlighten you on the most excellent way.

Chapter Nine

The Most Excellent Way—An Effective Approach to Bullying Prevention

I don't have a catchy name for it. If pressed, I would call it something like 'Growing communities of respect' or 'Creating Build Up Zones'.

I believe that the most effective approach to the bullying issue in schools is to prevent it from happening in the first place. To eliminate bullying, we need to create communities of respect, connectedness, positivity, and restorative practice.

The equation is simple:

More Respect = Less Bullying.

If there is more respect for each other, there will be less bullying.

We don't need more 'policies' about bullying, but practical solutions that create respectful community relationships, where emotional and relational health and well-being is utmost priority.

One school I visited had a large sign in their undercover/assembly area. Like the Ghostbusters sign, it had a large red circle and a diagonal line across the centre. Written on the sign were the words 'No Bullying'. A new parent asked the principal if there was a bullying problem at the school. The principal answered by saying, 'No. What made you ask the question?'

The parent mentioned the sign and said that it seemed negative and that it was sending a message that bullying was a problem in the school.

The principal was surprised, but agreed. The sign was removed.

This experience was one of the many that led me to think of more positive ways of tackling the bullying issue. I had once thought of placing on every child in the school a button badge that read 'No putdowns', as a way of tackling bullying. It occurred to me that this was also negative and might have an adverse effect. It's like saying, 'This is what I don't want you to do. Now, don't do it!' It's like saying to you, 'Don't think of pink elephants!' Couldn't help it, could you? I would much rather we said what we wanted, instead of what we don't want. It gives us something to aim at, something to strive for.

I then began to think about the opposite phrase to a 'Put Down'.

A 'Build Up'.

Ah ha! A Build Up Zone. This school is a Build Up Zone (BUZ) ®. I am a Build Up Zone. You are a Build Up Zone, our family is a Build Up Zone, our community is a Build Up Zone. I then set to work on developing what a Build Up Zone would look like.

Over time, at the school that had removed the 'No Bullying' sign, there was a reduction in bullying. This was due to a focus on building positive relationships and respect and instigating many of the early BUZ initiatives. This reduction was indicated by the school's 'bullying survey.'

Again, the school realised that the survey they were conducting was itself quite negative. It only asked negative questions, for example, 'Have you been hit, punched, and kicked?' 'Has anyone threatened you?' and so on. It wasn't long before a friendship survey was created, to monitor the positives in children's relationships.

After a few years, the school conducted a 'Best Practice' survey amongst the students. According to the national average of the results, the school scored very high in social skills. Ten years after this, I was speaking to a primary school chaplain. She told me that an education district director was doing an assessment at her school. He spoke with her about her work, and she had mentioned that she conducts some of the BUZ initiatives. In his response to her, he mentioned the school that scored high in the National Best Practice survey on social skills. Word had got out!

Here's another way to look at prevention of bullying:

If you want to decrease bullying in schools, don't pay a lot of attention to it.

It serves little purpose in bowing to the negativity of trying to find what is wrong and then fixing it. This is a pathological way of tacking an issue. It can't be classed as 'prevention'. Often, it is not even an effective cure.

BUZ practice is about finding what is good and making it better. It is about focusing on the future. It is not always an easy concept to get support for, because we humans are wired to find out what is wrong with something, plan a program to fix it, run the program, and then evaluate how well the program went.

It seems to me that the best way to fix something is to not let it get broken in the first place. Imagine if an airline company had a maintenance policy of only fixing something when it was broken!

Discard the Labels

I try not to use the terms 'bully' or 'victim' in my work and conversation with children and parents; they are usually not helpful labels.

I remember doing a BUZ show at a school. Halfway through the show, the deputy principal came backstage while I was changing costume (bit embarrassing). She asked if I could pick a particular boy in the audience who was a 'victim' to do something on the stage. She said it would be good for him. What an awful label—'victim'! By using this term, she perpetuated the stigma. I decided that it was best not to choose the child.

Having said this, I will however, in this book, occasionally use the term 'bully'. When I do, it is to abbreviate the term, 'A person who has violated the rights of another to feel safe and be respected.' If I use the term 'victim', it is to abbreviate the term, 'A person who has had their right to feel safe and be respected abused.' I will use the term 'bullying' to abbreviate the term, 'When a person (or persons) has violated the rights of another person to feel safe and be respected in a planned, persistent, and ongoing way.'

Chapter Ten

Balancing the Power

Bully-proofing is about empowering and building confidence. It is about balancing the power.

Bully-proofing is helping a child to learn the social skills to handle a situation where they feel that their right to feel safe and be respected has been abused.

In simplified language, 'When I feel picked on'.

Shaking off the Shackles

I first came across Chloe when a friend of hers came to see me about not getting along with her. I'll call the friend Phoebe. I brought Phoebe and Chloe together to do some conflict resolution. I thought it went well as the girls cried a little and said sorry to each other and that they wanted to be friends.

As I got to know Chloe more, I discovered she had some home issues that she needed some support with. She lived with her mum whom she fought with a lot. She adored her grandmother and grandfather whom mum fought with a lot. I also discovered that Chloe has some social issues. The best way to describe her was clumsy and like a bull in a China shop with her friendships.

She didn't have much trouble making friends, but she was unable to sustain friendships. As I talked with Chloe and helped her with some friendship skills, I began to see something else that was happening.

Nearly every child she made friends with came to me to complain that she had been bullying them. It seemed strange.

To cut a long story short, I did some investigating and listening to children, teachers, and parents. What I discovered was a culture of dislike for this child. As I could see, it started for her in pre-primary. My probing revealed that her mother had somehow offended a number of the pre-primary mothers. Chloe was kind of blacklisted by the mothers who encouraged their daughters not to be friends with her.

This carried on till year four when I first met Chloe. She had a reputation amongst the mothers as a 'bully'. I admit that she was sometimes clumsy with her friendships, and she sometimes lacked the finesse involved in the intricacies of pre-adolescent girls. All of the other children were sometimes forgiving. They actually wanted to be friends with Chloe. This was encouraging, but the parents were not encouraging. Most parents were still telling their children not to have anything to do with her.

I remember walking through the school playground one day alongside a parent. She pointed to Chloe and said something like this, 'That's the girl who is the bully. She is so tall that she even intimidates me!' I couldn't believe what I was hearing. Here was a grown adult saying that she was the one who felt intimidated. Chloe was tall for her age, but really that had nothing to do with it.

I had grown a tremendous respect for Chloe and wanted to stick up for her. I can't remember exactly what I said, possibly something like this, 'Chloe is actually a great person. I've been helping her with some friendship issues. She has changed a lot, and you would be surprised how well she treats other children now.'

The parent said, 'I have noticed that she is a bit different. My daughter has actually asked if she could come for a play date. Now that you have said this I think I might give it a go.'

'Yeeeesss! Thank goodness, this parent was prepared to buck the social stigma!'

Chloe came to see me one day. She was visually upset. She showed me her iPad and the post that someone had put on her 'Moshi Monster' wall. Two of her classmates had got together and posted a note that said something like, 'Our mums said that if you are not nice to us, we can bully you for ten days!'

Through the tears, Chloe sobbed out the words, 'I think I am being bullied.'

Because it was outside of school hours and because it was a cyber bullying issue, it was right for me to follow the school procedure for this kind of thing. This meant contacting the parents of the girls who posted the note. I let the girls know that I was going to do this. They were both very upset, but I thought it was right that the parents knew.

The mother of one of the girls was away, and she begged me not to tell her dad because she said that he gets too angry, but to wait until mum came home. I obliged.

I bumped into the other mother the next day, and we spoke about her daughter's post on Chloe's wall. She was apologetic. She hadn't realised that her daughter was actually going to say the words on the post. She did confess that it was probably not a helpful thing to say to her daughter.

Unfortunately, she was perpetuating the myth that Chloe was a 'bully'. When I spoke to the mother who was away at the time, she was quite good about it and said that she will speak to her daughter about the incident. The girls all came together for a restorative session and resolved some of their differences.

It was a difficult process to help Chloe lose the label, the social stigma, the reputation. It seems like every time we were getting somewhere and she was beginning to make friends, something or someone was sabotaging the relationships. This is where Phoebe comes back into the picture.

One day, out of the blue Phoebe came to see me. It was towards the end of the year, and she was leaving the school. During the session, she was very upset as she told me that she was sorry for the way she had treated Chloe. She told me that every time Chloe made a friend, she would make friends with the same girl and in time tell them lots of bad things about Chloe. She also said that she got the friends to be mean to Chloe.

I had my suspicions but didn't want to ever accuse her of doing this very thing, but here, she was confessing it to me. I asked her why she was telling me this and owning up to it. I remember the look of sheer honesty and integrity on her face and the deep sincerity in her voice as she spoke these words, 'I decided that I wanted to be a better person.'

I choked up and was moved to tears. I always had respect for Phoebe, but that day it grew hundredfold.

Slowly, over time, the shackles of Chloe's reputation fell loose.

Chloe was accepted into a group of the popular girls. She still has her tiffs on occasions.

Izzy Kalman from www.bullies2buddies.com defines bullying as *'wrong relationships,* in other words, a lack of respect for each other.' He also says, *'The modern world failed to teach morality, kindness and love'.*

As I am writing this, I am in a cafe near a children's playground. I hear the following words ringing out, 'Ha, ha, you're a loser!' I look up to see two boys about seven years old standing on the wall making interesting hand signals to a girl about the same age. It was the girl, in her pretty pink dress, piggy tails, and ribbons calling out the words, 'Ha, ha, you're a loser!' Classic! She chased them, and they played their game. I wonder how David Attenborough would commentate on this primitive human behaviour.

Conflict Vs Bullying

Way back in my early experiences of working with children, a group of girls was having some problems with bullying amongst each other. Some of their parents were making regular visits to the school to get it sorted out. It seemed that each week, a different girl was being bullied. I offered to help out.

I met with the girls. At first, it was a bit of a scary experience. There were seven of them involved. I asked them, 'When did this problem first start?'

One of the girls said, 'At the beginning of last year'.

This meant that the problem had been ongoing for eighteen months.

She went on to say, 'It started when Leonie (one of the girls) first came to the school.'

The others agreed, including Leonie, who wasn't offended by the suggestion.

After some discussion, each of the girls agreed that they had not only been picked on, but that each had picked on others. What I came to realise was that these girls were in conflict with each other, mostly because their social group had lost its balance and the girls lacked the skills to resolve their initial and some subsequent conflict.

For this group of girls, whenever two of them had a disagreement, they were unable to solve the problem, so they tried to get the others on their side. This always led to an imbalance of power; hence, in the mind of the parents, bullying was occurring.

Together, the girls and I worked on a positive set of outcomes that they could work towards. One of the strategies was to learn some conflict resolution skills. If these girls had developed these skills earlier, then ongoing conflict may not have evolved into bullying.

I came to discover that most bullying occurs because children are unable to solve conflict. They feel powerless when a friendship problem arises and eventually someone gets the upper hand.

I am so grateful to that group of girls. By listening to them, they taught me a tremendous amount about relationships. They helped me with ideas and were my guinea pigs for the first batch of 'BUZ Helps Cards'.

It's interesting to note that all, bar one of these girls had experienced a family breakdown.

The Secret

A seven-year-old girl, Erin, came to see me because she was upset that a friend of hers, Alli, told a boy one of her secrets. When I asked if she was able to tell me what the secret was, she said, 'Alli told him that I said he was a bully.'

I asked her what he did. She said that he was mean to her and that he is often mean to her. What is interesting is that she said that Alli had bullied her as well. I asked her how. She said by telling the boy her secret.

Later, when I had the two girls together, Erin was telling Alli how she felt about what happened.

Alli replied, 'I said to him that he should stop bullying you. I was standing up for you.'

I was sad to hear these girls just throwing the word bully and bullying around as if anything that happened in conflict was 'bullying'. Erin originally said that she didn't want to be Alli's friend anymore because she told people her secrets. They were best friends. This was a misunderstanding between the girls and originally they didn't have a chance to tell each other how they felt. We owe it to children to allow them opportunities to resolve conflict and equip them with the skills to do it. It doesn't help if we use the word 'bullying' willy-nilly every time children are treated meanly by another.

Years ago, children hardly used the word 'bully'. Parents tend to heighten children's awareness to bullying by throwing every negative thing that happens in children's relationships in the 'bullying basket'. This makes it difficult for children to delineate between what is true bullying and what is conflict.

Chapter Eleven

Social Confidence

I recently had the good fortune to go on a cruise. I took the potluck dinner seating option where you can meet different people each evening. On one occasion, I sat next to an amazing retired lady who was about to become a great-grandmother for the first time.

She said to me that it's a tough world to be bringing up children.

I said that I thought it was an amazing world where children have so much to look forward to.

She disagreed with me and said that children had to contend with serious things like bullying.

I asked her if she thought bullying was really bad or whether the media just beat it up.

She said that her granddaughters had to move schools because of bullying.

I asked her, 'What would you say if I told you that bullying is no worse than it was when you were a child?'

She sternly said, 'Oh, no, it is much worse.'

I wanted to challenge her but in a way that she wouldn't become defensive. I didn't want to lecture her or patronise her. I wanted to be sensitive, tactful, but honest. She didn't know much about me, and she didn't know I was writing a book about the issue.

How was I to sum up this book in one dinner conversation? Here was my chance to practice.

I said something like this, 'Remember I told you that I work with children, developing social and emotional well-being?'

'Yes'. I had gained her interest.

'One of the areas I specialise in is bullying. In fact, I am currently working on a new book.'

I had a gut feeling that her granddaughters were now in their teen years but had to move schools late in their primary years. I suppose I had this feeling because this is a common scenario I come across. I also made the assumption that earlier in their primary years, the girls' family had broken down.

I continued, 'In my book, I suggest that most bulling between girls starts from conflict that doesn't get resolved. I'm guessing that your granddaughters were being bullied by girls who used to be their friends.'

'Yes.' She nodded. I could see her grasping that reality, wondering how I knew.

'What I usually encounter in my experience is that there is some sort of disagreement and one of the girls who is going through some other grief issues in their life at the time loses some of their social confidence and feels powerless as the other child gains power in the conflict.'

I looked at the great-grandmother to be, and I could see the welling up of tears in her eyes. 'How old are your granddaughters?' I asked.

'Fifteen and eighteen'.

'How old were they when this bullying happened, when they changed schools?'

'In primary school.'

'Did they have some grief issues in their life at the time?'

She looked at me as if to say, 'He's hit the nail on the head.'

'Their mum and dad broke up when they were five and eight.'

She went on to say that it was a messy break up followed by years of court appearances etc.

I said that the girls would have gone through a lot of grief at the time and that grief has a powerful way of reducing their social confidence. Because of this, it made the girls more vulnerable in conflict with their friends, and my guess is that the girls first started talking about how mean their friends were getting, until the time when it appeared to be full-blown bullying. This is where a decision was made to take the girls to a new school.

'Amazing, that's pretty much what happened!' She looked at me like I had just amazed her with a magic trick.

So I asked her, 'Does that give you a different perspective on bullying?'

'I certainly see it differently now.'

The other people at the table were listening intently to the whole conversation.

As I looked up at them, I could see a small group of people who had discovered a new way of looking at an age old problem. I went on to say that this doesn't explain all of the bullying that happens, but it does help us to get a perspective on the kind of issues that are at stake.

We continued our conversation around marriage breakdown, relationships, conflict resolution, and social confidence. She also talked more about her new great-granddaughter to be, the mother being the eighteen-year-old granddaughter.

The dinner was a contradiction. The 'reef and beef' was polarised in more ways than one. The steak was scrumptious, but the lobster was undercooked, chewy, and soggy, needless to say I suffered a little later. The dessert redeemed the occasion, but I think I had a chocolate overdose. Three extra laps around the deck!

I came away from the dinner and the conversation with the words 'social confidence' running around in my brain. If I was forced to summarise bully-proofing into two words, I would probably say 'social confidence'.

Martin Seligman talks about this 'social confidence' in his book *The Optimistic Child*.

> Children with good social and problem solving skills make new friends. They are comfortable in new situations. They say hello to children they have not met before and join in novel activities. They also know how to maintain friendships. They cooperate. They compromise. They trust others, and others trust in them. Children with good social and problem solving skills handle conflicts well. They respect differences. They state their wishes clearly and assertively. They apologize when they are wrong, but they stick to their guns when they are right.

I love this description of a socially confident child. It gives us a distinct list of social skills that we would wish for children to possess. Children with these skills know how to handle friendship stuff. They still need our support, but they know when and how to get it. It is part of their problem-solving skills.

Chapter Twelve

Used to Be Friends

I am staggered at the number of bullying incidents between children who used to be best friends. This has led me to the conclusion that most bullying is caused by festering, unresolved conflict between children.

I viewed a documentary movie called 'Bully'. It is an interesting movie that I remain indifferent about. It sensationalises 'bullying' in a way that I don't think is helpful. You be the judge if you ever get a chance to see it.

In one part of the movie, a group of early adolescent children are walking into the school hallway after a break. On the way in, a teacher stops two boys. Obviously, there had been an issue between the boys. It became apparent that one boy had been bullying the other. The body language was interesting. As the teacher spoke with the boys, one (the perpetrator) was standing confidently and looking cocky; the other was standing in a slouched and weak stance with his head down.

Here is my recollection of the encounter.

The teacher said to the cocky boy, 'Now, I think you should say sorry to . . . (Name).'

To which the boy put out his hand to the other boy and said a contrived, 'Sorry.'

The slouched boy didn't respond.

The teacher said to him, 'Come on, now you can see that . . . (Name) is offering his apology, what is wrong with you?'

The boy answered, 'I'm not accepting his apology. He always treats me like this. He says sorry, but doesn't mean it.'

The teacher said something about why couldn't he be like the other boy.

She dismissed the boy who was trying to say sorry.

After he left, she said to the boy who was being stubborn about not accepting the apology, 'Why can't you just accept his apology and just be friends?'

To which the boy made a deep sigh and sternly replied through gritted teeth, 'That's the problem. We used to be friends!'

Unfortunately, the teacher just wasn't getting it. Even after the incident when the teacher was being interviewed, she was still totally oblivious to the real issue, and she was incompetent in the way she handled the incident. She thought she was doing a great service by trying to get the boy to accept what was obviously an insincere apology. I was quite disturbed by the scene.

Chapter Thirteen

Power Imbalance

I asked a sixteen-year-old girl, 'Were you ever bullied as a child?'

'Yes, by one girl, from year two to year four. She used to hit me a lot and be really mean to me. I remember telling the teachers about it, I suppose getting her in trouble. When I look back on it now, I don't think the teachers handled it very well. The girl needed some help. She had a lot of problems at home, and I guess she was bringing those problems to school and taking them out on me.'

'Knowing what you know now, would you have handled it any differently?'

'Yes. I would have stood up to her more and not let her have power over me.'

'Was this girl your friend?'

'Yes, but she made me play with her.'

'How did it stop in year four?'

'She got into trouble, and she had to leave the school.'

'Did you feel bad about that?'

'No, I was happy. I feel a bit bad now. I wish she was able to get some help. She wasn't a bad person. I saw her recently and talked to her about it. She said to me that she couldn't believe that she used to treat me like that.'

'Did she say sorry?'

'She didn't actually say the word "sorry", but I think she was.'

I liked the integrity of this sixteen-year-old. I especially liked the way she said that knowing what she knew now she wouldn't have let the girl have power over her.

We all have a tendency to feel bullied when we feel powerless or when we are in conflict with someone and we don't know what to do about it.

Empowering the person who feels like a victim (or powerless) can often disempower the bully (the person with the power). Another way of putting this is to balance the power by helping the person who feels powerless to have confidence, a sense of hope, and the resolve to handle difficult social situations, 'social confidence'.

At the bully-proofing parent workshops I conduct, I ask the question, 'When your child has been bullied at school, what do they usually say to you when they come home?' The answers include, 'Tommy keeps hurting me.' 'Sally won't let me join in.' 'So and so is being mean.'

After some discussion, we discovered that children rarely come home and say, 'I was bullied today.'

The words 'bully' or 'bullying' are not really part of a young primary-aged child's vocabulary. They are adult words. More recently, it is unfortunately becoming a word that many children are tending to lean towards when someone is not nice to them.

The most regular comment I hear when children feel powerless is 'They were *mean* to me.'

What does mean, mean?

I have discovered that, in a child's mind, when someone is being mean to them, it usually suggests that the other person has said or done something that hurt their feelings. In other words, they had a negative reaction to a social encounter and felt uncomfortable, possibly angry, disappointed, and sad or rejected. Real feelings—that are not always easy to handle. The child is coming to grips with feeling this way and usually blames the other child for their uncomfortable feelings.

'You did this to me.' In other words, 'You were mean to me.' In a child's mind, this indicates a power imbalance. They don't know what to do. They feel disempowered.

Chapter Fourteen

Repowering

Listen and Validate Feelings—A Good Starting Point

One of the best things we can do to help children overcome a situation where they feel picked on or powerless is to help them handle their feelings. In my book *BUZology*, I develop this further. In chapters on the 'Feelings Management Creed', 'Agro and Emo—riding the emotional roller coaster', and 'Anger Management', I delve into the world of emotional competence.

I picked up a book in a bookstall once. I think it was titled, *How to Help Your Kids*. I opened it. The first page had a single word, 'Listen'. I turned the page, 'Listen'. I turned the page again, 'Listen.' The fourth page said, 'If you haven't got it by now . . . the best way to help your kids is to listen.'

Good listening or active listening involves validating feelings. One of the best gifts we can give to our children is to help them understand their feelings and handle their emotions. Helping them express the way they feel about something empowers them with a valuable life skill.

In my early days, as I worked in schools and on camps, children would often come up to me to tell me that someone was being mean to them or picking on them. I would assume that they wanted my help without me actually asking them if they did. Something inside of me would trigger and I would go into action and try and fix it up, imagining myself as Clint Eastwood. Must have been the testosterone kicking in.

'Right', I would say, 'no one is going to pick on you.' I would go over to the other child to see if I could fix it up. Lo and behold, it was never a simple case of bullying; there was always some kind of conflict involved. There was often a power imbalance and one child would get upset.

I made the mistake of assuming that because a child was telling me about what happened that they wanted my help. I started asking the question, 'Do you want my help?' I was surprised that in less than half of the situations, children actually wanted direct help. Usually, they just wanted someone to hear how they were feeling and to have their feelings validated, and then they would get themselves back into the friendship ring for another round.

Here are some suggested responses you could use for when your child tells you they have been picked on, hurt, or bullied.

What happened?

How do you feel?

That must have been hard or hurtful for you.

Would you like my help?

What have you tried so far?

What else could you try?

Are you hurt?

Have you got some ideas to handle this?

Do you feel safe now?

What else can you do to feel safe?

A single mother was telling me about her ten-year-old son and his father. The son was being picked on by a group of boys at soccer. They were boys from his school. The father decided that he was going to do something about it, without the son's permission.

He went down to the soccer field and spoke to the boys. The son came home very upset with his father for doing so. He didn't want his dad to interfere.

The next day, the son came home looking taller than usual. He went to his dad and said, 'Dad, even though you did the wrong thing by talking to the boys who were picking on me, at least I felt you supported me, and that gave me the courage to talk to the boys myself, and they won't be picking on me anymore.'

I looked at the mother as she was telling this story, and tears were streaming down her cheeks.

So, if you want to help your kids, support them. Listen to them, validate their feelings, and ask them if they need your help. You could also help them to decide whether the situation is actually bullying or a conflict. Empowering your child's conflict resolution skills will equip them to deal with some of the trickiest relationship issues.

Chapter Fifteen

The Skill of Conflict Resolution

One of the most effective inoculations against bullying is the skill of conflict resolution.

Children learn most of their conflict resolution skills at home. If you and your spouse/partner are experiencing conflict, the way you handle it will have a direct effect on your child and their relationship skills, in other words, their 'social confidence'.

I have observed over the years that children whose parents break up when they are between the ages of three to five seem to have the most difficulty in relationship skills and conflict resolution. There must be some important brain development during these early years that is affected or even underdeveloped when there is conflict at home.

Marriages usually don't break up overnight; they take three to five years to get to the point when a couple decides to go their own ways. This has meant that for the first three to five years of a child's life, they have been exposed to conflict in the home. I would love to see some solid research on this.

My other observation is that children who are exposed to parents who continue to have intense conflict after separation also struggle with their social confidence.

Children experience conflict in all aspects of their lives, and one of the greatest gifts that we can give them is to teach them how to live with and resolve conflict. It is not totally realistic to stop children having any conflict with others, but it is sensible to gift them with the ability to resolve conflict and solve problems.

In their book, *Best Friends, Worst Enemies*, Michael Thompson, Catherine O'Neill Grace, and Lawrence J. Cohen say that children are driven by three basic needs: power, recognition, and connection, and that as they struggle to fulfil these needs, they inevitably come into conflict with their classmates.

Conflict happens. Conflict is a normal part of life. Different beliefs, different customs, different expectations, and different ideas mean that people will often come into conflict.

Bullying is a form of conflict, but usually infers that one party has the upper hand, therefore creating a power imbalance.

When children are given the opportunity to learn the skills of conflict resolution, they will have important skills for the rest of their lives. The BUZ Hopscotch Method of Conflict Resolution © is a very effective process for helping children resolve conflict with their peers, family, and friends. In the book *BUZology*, I give a full description of the process and its workings. Here, is a brief version.

The BUZ Hopscotch Method of Conflict Resolution ©

1. Stop and Think

When I teach this step with children and adults, I ask the following questions:

'What is the main feeling expressed in a fight?'

'Anger.'

'What colour do we normally think of when we think of anger?'

'Red.'

'What colour is a stop sign?'

'Red.'

'What do we do when we come to a stop sign?'

'Stop!'

'What happens if we don't?'

'We could crash! Or we would get in trouble.'

The same could happen when we are in a fight with someone if we don't stop and think. This stopping and thinking allows time to cool down and think about 'what happened' and how we are feeling. This is an important part of feelings management. Know how you feel and know why you feel that way.

Feelings management is the springboard for diving into the depths of conflict resolution. It allows one or both people to be calm enough to say to each other, 'Can we talk about this?'

2. Talk and Listen

The next step is to talk. Communicate with each other by saying how you feel and why you feel that way. This is best done using 'I messages'. A 'you message' is usually interpreted as blaming and creates a barrier to communication. An 'I message' is less threatening. It allows the speaker to say how they are feeling about what happened.

When a person says how they feel, it is a moment of openness.

'I felt angry when the ball was taken from me!' (Example of an 'I message'.)

'You made me angry when you stole the ball off me.' (Example of a 'you message'.)

'I am sad that you called me that.' (I message.)

'You are so mean to say that to me.' (You message.)

When a person says how they feel first, it is more honest and helpful than saying what the other person did. This creates awareness and an opening to hear the other person out. Both need to talk, and equally, both need to listen. It is much easier to listen to someone who is open and honest than someone who is closed and blaming. Listening also allows each person to hear how the other person is feeling, which is an important component of the skill of empathy.

When I am mediating between children, I find that when they get to this point, the rest seems to go so smoothly. Once they have heard how the other feels and they have an element of empathy, there is an openness to want to resolve the conflict.

Eye contact is an important part of this. When I lead children through conflict resolution, I get them to face each other, so they can see each other's eyes. Talking is only a small part of real communication. There is a tremendous amount of research around in the brain science world on 'mirroring'. This is about one person listening to another, seeing in the other person's eyes the full message and the emotions involved in the message. This triggers parts of their own brains to light up, and empathy can occur.

3. Problem

The next component is to find the cause of the conflict (problem). All other problems stem from the original problem. Sometimes conflict between children has a chain reaction or domino effect. If the original problem can be discovered, then it makes it so much easier to resolve the conflict.

Remember, a problem is a problem. It is not helpful to consider that a person is the problem. A problem can however be created by a person's behaviour.

When children are trying to find the problem, they often confuse the problem with what happened. For example, if two children are fighting over a ball, what children will often say the problem is 'We are fighting over a ball.'

'That is what is happening. What caused you to fight over the ball?'

'We both wanted the ball.'

'How many balls are there?'

'One!'

The penny drops. 'The problem is that there is only one ball and two people and both want it.'

I have come to discover that most conflict between children can be defined as what I call the '1 to 2'. There is usually one thing, idea, way, game, etc, and there are usually two people, both wanting the same thing, their idea, their way, their game, etc.

4. Ideas (to fix the problem)

Once the problem has been identified, it is easier to find a solution, obviously, but not always easy.

Originally, I was thinking of a ladder model as I was working on the conflict resolution process; however, when I reached this point, I realised that I needed two squares. This is where it became apparent that I was now creating a hopscotch template. This came about because I realised that there may be more than one way to fix a problem.

There are two people, and both may have different ideas that will lead to a resolution. Both need to be able to contribute their ideas. If the problem has been defined well and the two are in tune with each other, the first idea can be the best. When two people have different ideas, then both need to work together and negotiate. Before they can move to the next square, they need to reach a compromise on their ideas so as to find an agreeable solution, where there is a 'win-win' situation.

All ideas should be allowed on the table, even ideas you may not like. It is best to say, 'That's an idea.' than to say, 'That's a bad idea.'

5. Agree and Fix

By this stage, they should be able to agree on the solution and put it into practice. Both need to make a decision on the action needed and to act upon it. If it hasn't occurred already, this is where you may see children actually say sorry to each other voluntarily, without prompting. It is a relief for them as they can see a solution to something that brought them grief. They are both empowered. The power balance is restored. They are aware of their own actions which may not have been helpful and are genuinely sorry.

6. Celebrate

Because I had now decided on the hopscotch template, I had to think about the 'home' base. After the work involved in resolving the conflict, both people can enjoy a restored relationship and that is worth celebrating. When I mediate for children, I often get to this point and ask, 'How will you celebrate?'

'By playing together again!' is a common answer.

When I first developed the Hopscotch Method of Conflict Resolution, I had no idea of the potential impact. I now realise that it is essential for social skills. It is the central and crucial component. I discovered that all major social skills are needed to resolve conflict.

On many occasions, I have presented the BUZ Hopscotch Method of Conflict Resolution to gatherings of parents. A question I often get asked is 'When should we teach this to our children?'

I usually answer something like this, 'The moment they are born. They are already learning from you the moment they take their first breath and even earlier in the womb. Whenever you have conflict with someone, they are observing and learning.'

'For good or for ill, you are already teaching children your conflict resolution skills.'

Chapter Sixteen

Should We Make Children Say Sorry to Each Other?

When I teach the BUZ Hopscotch Method to children, I have large place mats for each step that I place on the floor. After we have been through the process, I bring out a card with the word 'sorry' on it. I ask them to place the card on the Hopscotch in the position they think it belongs. It is a very interesting exercise that creates some amazing discussion.

Together we discover that it can go anywhere. The main reason for this is that the process itself is a way of saying sorry. The process is what is important, not the word. The word is certainly helpful, but on its own, it doesn't mean much. The BUZ Hopscotch Method of Conflict Resolution is reconciliation at its best.

One of my pet hates is when children are told or forced to say sorry to each other, as if the word will magically fix the problem. I often ask children if they have ever meant it, when they were told by adults to say sorry to each other.

'No!' is always the resounding answer. They go on to say that they hate it when adults tell them to say sorry.

I usually find when children are given the opportunity to respectfully sort out their conflicts, they will naturally come to say sorry to the other person, even if they have only done a small thing wrong in their own eyes. They don't need prompting.

'It takes courage to say sorry.'

I often ask groups of children, 'What usually goes with sorry to complete it?'

'Forgiveness!' is their answer.

I ask them what forgiveness is and get an interesting collection of answers, most of which are about accepting the apology and restoring the friendship. I am sincerely amazed at the power of forgiveness, especially when children embrace it. They are masters of being friends again.

I once asked two girls how they fixed the fight they were having. They said, 'We just started playing together again.'

'Forgiveness is a great way to start over again. It is the glue that repairs a broken friendship.'

Chapter Seventeen

A Conflict Resolution Case Study

Three 8-year-old children were getting some help from me for a fight they had been having amongst themselves, one girl and two boys. The girl had invited one of the boys to join her 'spying club'. She was honest enough to say that she invited him because she thought he would be the only one to join.

However, she had invited another boy also. She liked this other boy more and told the first boy that he could no longer be in the club. Some would say that this is bullying.

I worked through the conflict with them in my usual fashion using the Hopscotch Method. The three children had been taught this in their class in a BUZ program. They were very honest and sensible as they worked through each step with me. I didn't tell them that we were actually using the Hopscotch Method. I just did it.

When we reached the 'Ideas' step, the girl pointed up at the hopscotch poster on my wall and said, 'We're up to here.' She had been following our progress with precision.

An interesting development happened towards the end. The two boys were up and about dancing around and giving each other high fives. She was annoyed with them. I said to her that the boys had reached the 'Celebrate' step.

She said strongly, 'I haven't!'

She was still at the 'agree and fix' stage. The boys saw how to fix the problem, but they didn't get the nod of approval from the girl.

The solution to the problem meant that she had the most at stake and she was still coming to grips with that. She still didn't want the first boy to be her friend because of some other outstanding issues. These included that their parents didn't like each other, and this played on the mind of the girl. She wanted to be loyal to her mum. She began talking about how strict her parents were and tears welled up in her eyes. She had the attention and sympathy of the boys and together they all shared stories of different parenting styles.

Eventually, after dealing with the emotions associated with the parents, she was calmer and more open to the boys' ideas. They all agreed to not have 'clubs' but to just play together and to help with the 'two's company and three's a crowd syndrome'; they decided they would get another child to play with them.

Chapter Eighteen

Mate-Ship and Rivalry

In my primary school years, I had a great mate. His name was Alex. We were friends all the way through our primary years. I loved going to his house after school. He had a TV, we didn't. His mum used to fry a piece of bread in dripping, (not on a health conscious school canteen menu nowadays). We would sit down to eat it in front of the Mickey Mouse Club.

It was great friendship. Did we ever fight? All of the time. I think we were always trying to be better than each other, especially at the physical stuff. We would rumble and tumble a lot. I think we used to fight every second day. There were times I got so mad with him, but he was a mate. It was always a power struggle between us. I don't think it was a bad thing. I think it is quite normal for boys (and girls in a different way) to have rivalry. After all, we are members of the animal kingdom. Whether we like it or not, it is in our DNA. Conflict is inevitable between people, even or especially friends. It's the outcome of the conflict that matters. I wish I knew then what I know now.

From the beginning of the human race, there has always been tension and conflict in relationships. We can't escape it, but we can escape the ugly face of unresolved or badly handled conflict, especially that which turns into bullying.

'Children are desperate to learn conflict resolution skills. It is one thing for them to make friends. To hold on to friends is another.'

In a child's language, 'I want to keep friends.'

Chapter Nineteen

Genuine Bullying

Does genuine bullying actually happen? You bet. I've seen people of all ages treat others with total disregard and lack of respect.

There is a reason the following words exist in our vocabulary: Hate, bigotry, racism, malice, greed, prejudice, intolerance, hostility, abuse, violence, and war. The reason is because unfortunately, they happen. Each of these is about lack of respect for other people.

Bullying fits in alongside of these things. There are two basic ways of handling bullying. One is to stop everyone in the world from bullying. The other is to learn how to handle it. We can't really control the first one, but we can certainly do a lot with the second.

Unfortunately, we don't live in a perfect world. There will always be people who don't respect others. Our children need resilience and the ability to stand up to wrongdoing, evil, and hatred. Equipping kids to be strong in the face of adversity is part of life. We may not be able to change the actions of others, but we can certainly change the way we respond to them. This embraces maintaining our dignity and sense of self.

In relation to bullying, we may not be able to stop it, but we can certainly act when it happens to ourselves, our friends, and our family.

> *If I was king of USA I would make it so that there was no popularity—that everyone was equal.*

(A quote from a boy in the movie 'Bully'.)

Shoes in the Rafters

This is the story I alluded to in chapter one. When I was in high school, I remember this one boy who used to pick on me a lot. Not sure why. I didn't like the way he treated me. Looking back on it now, this was a bullying experience for me. The best way to describe the boy is that he was arrogant. A bit of a knob! Am I allowed to use that word?

I remember one day after sport, looking for my shoes. He had thrown them in the rafters. I had enough! As I tried to get them down, I think he tried to stop me or something. All I remember was losing my cool and swinging my fists around. Somehow it connected him on the jaw and flattened him.

Now, I am far from a violent person and was totally shocked at my actions. It wasn't even a conscious effort to stand up to for myself. I think I just snapped.

Some other kids were watching on. I can't remember seeing any reaction from them. All I know is that I got my shoes down, and after that incident, he never picked on me again. I think I know the science of what happened.

I will never forget it. I didn't feel good about myself for doing it, but I was pleased that he didn't pick on me anymore. I just wish there was another way I could have handled it at the time.

Chapter Twenty

School Policies on Bullying and Options for Children

Many schools have policies on bullying. In most states, it is a requirement by their various education departments. Most of these policies include some kind of process that children are meant to use when they are being bullied at school. Here is a list of the options that children are often presented with in the majority of schools.

If you are being bullied you can:

- o Walk away
- o Tell them to stop
- o Tell a teacher

Let me explain why most of the time these are ineffective, that children themselves generally don't like them and say that they don't work!

When a child comes to talk to me about being picked on, teased, or bullied by someone, I ask them, 'What have you tried so far?' To which most of them say one or more of the following:

'I walked away, but they followed me.'

'They are in my class, and I can't get away from them.'

'I told them to stop, but they just keep on doing it'.

'I have tried telling a teacher, but they don't do anything'.

These are the most common responses I get from children. They do not at all feel empowered by the strategies that schools are presenting to them.

Let me unpack each, one at a time.

Walk Away

Whilst this can be a useful strategy, children are not being taught how and when to use it properly.

When I first started working in schools and even now, many years later, the most common response that teachers and parents say to children when they complain about how another child has treated them is, 'We'll, don't play with them.' Or 'Stay away from them'.

Remember, most of the time, bullying comes from unresolved conflict. Staying away or walking away from someone is not going to solve conflict; it usually serves to make it worse. One of the BUZ posters says, 'If you have a fight with a friend, *talk*, don't walk'.

Many children tell me that they want to sort out a disagreement, but the other person just keeps walking away. They are extremely frustrated by this and feel helpless when the other child just walks away.

Tell Them to Stop

When I ask children about this one, they say, 'I have tried it, but it doesn't work.'

I usually ask them, 'So you spoke to them. What did you say?'

They usually say something like this, 'I said to them, "Can you please stop"'.

'That's nice. Did it work?'

'No!'

'Then why do you keep on using it? It seems to me that if someone is not treating you with respect, it would make more sense to speak firmly instead of nicely'.

They usually agree with me. Sometimes they say, 'I said to them, "Stop it. I don't like it"'.

'I've heard that before. Does that work?'

'No'.

'Where did you learn to say that?'

'In pre-primary! It's stupid Steve, but it's what teachers expect us to say. Everyone knows that it is dumb and it doesn't work'.

I know what they are talking about. As I understand, this strategy comes from protective behaviours and that is where it belongs. Children need a strong language when they are confronted with a situation where they need to protect themselves. If an adult is trying to touch them inappropriately, then they need to be able to say in a strong voice, 'Stop it. I don't like it'. It is an effective skill to protect children, but shouldn't be used in common conflict, teasing, and disagreements that children have with each other.

It is not respectful to the other child. Imagine if your spouse didn't like something you did and they said to you in a firm voice, with their hand thrust at you, 'Stop it. I don't like it'.

Whenever I give my talk on bully-proofing to early childhood teachers about this, it gets an interesting reaction. Many are lowering their heads. As I ask them about this, I have heard them say things like, 'I've never really liked getting children to say this' or 'Finally, someone is brave enough to tell us that this strategy is not really working.'

Let's face it, true bullying does not really happen in pre-primary. Children at this age are still developing their social and emotional brains, and the definition of bullying that I use at the beginning of the book just doesn't fit in early childhood. Don't get me wrong, children do have conflict at this age. This is the age we should be concentrating some powerful and practical social and emotional skills training. We owe these children a lot more than, 'Stop it. I don't like it'.

Tell a Teacher

When I ask children if they have told a teacher, by far the most common responses I get from children is either, 'They don't do anything' or 'I don't want to dob'.

When children say that the teachers don't do anything, they usually mean that the situation doesn't get better. I tell them that it doesn't mean that the teacher doesn't care. I know they do. I say to the child that often a teacher has so many children bringing these kinds of things to them that they feel a bit overwhelmed.

I ask them, 'What do teachers say to you when you speak to them about someone who is not treating you with respect?'

They respond with these kinds of answers; Sometimes they say to stay away from them. Sometimes they tell the other person off. Sometimes they say, 'Don't dob'.

I ask children what the difference between telling a teacher and dobbing is.

In a child's mind, 'They are the same!'

Some schools use, 'Get help' instead of 'Tell a teacher', but often these schools don't always teach children how to get help and when to get help. Often the teachers deal with the issue in a punitive way, which I have eluded to the shortcomings in earlier chapters. Sometimes teachers haven't been trained to handle conflict resolution and restorative practices between children, so the system falls down and children are frustrated and underpowered. The sixteen-year-old I mentioned earlier who said she was bullied by one girl between year two and four said to me, 'Teachers don't handle these things very well. They need more training on better ways.'

So, what are the skills that children need to learn? Read on. Star Trekkin' across the universe.

Chapter Twenty-One

Star Trek and Bully-Proofing

Allow me to indulge in a little Star Trek analogy.

Around the time I was first starting to think of developing these strategies for bully-proofing, I was watching an episode of *Star Trek*. The USS Starship Enterprise was being attacked by a rogue Klingon *Bird of Prey* attack vessel. Captain Picard followed the United Federation of Planets Protocol and the Prime Directive to a tee.

The first option the captain used was to put the ship into warp speed and depart from that particular quadrant. Just when they had cleared off, the *Bird of Prey* attack vessel decloaked right in front of the Starship and began attacking again.

The second option that Picard attempted was to communicate with the Klingons. Following procedure, Captain Picard opened the hailing frequencies and brought up the visual of the Klingon captain on the big screen.

'You are firing on a Federation Starship. We are on a peaceful mission. You must cease your hostile intent upon this vessel.'

The Klingon captain said something aggressive in Klingon and his image disappeared from the screen, followed by some more photon attacks.

Picard's third option was to fire a warning shot at the Klingons to show that they could match their power. This was done in the hope that the Klingons would back off. This, of course came after the usual warning, 'If you don't stop firing at us, we will be forced to defend ourselves.' Except spoken in more official Trekki kind of language.

One other option that Picard considered was to see if there were any other Federation Starships in the area, thinking that reinforcements might show the Klingons that there is strength in numbers. Unfortunately, the closest was some light years away. Even with wormholes and warp speed, they could not arrive in time.

The final option was for the Starship Enterprise to deploy the deflector shields, thus placing a force field around the ship for protection. For some reason or another, in every episode, the shields are prevented from reaching full power. I remember in the earlier episodes, when Captain Kirk would ask Scottie to increase power to the shields, the classic response in a broad Scottish accent was, 'But, capt'n, I'm givin'r all she's got'. Power would always need to be diverted from somewhere on the ship. Eventually, the shields would get back to near full strength, and it would save the day.

Nearly every episode of *Star Trek* I have seen, where the Enterprise was attacked, they would use these strategies to overcome the situation. They would use not just one, but a combination or all of the strategies.

Let me summarise the options that Captains Picard and Kirk used:

1. *Get Away*—Navigate the ship to a safe sector. (If you're not there, they can't shoot you)

2. *Communicate*—Open the communication channels. (Talk it out—the diplomatic option)
3. *Retaliate*—Fire a warning blast from the ship. (We can defend ourselves.)
4. *Reinforcements*—Call on other alliance ships in the vicinity. (Strength in numbers.)
5. *Force Field*—Deploy the ship's deflector shields and place a force field around the ship for protection. (Strengthen the defences.)

As I contemplated these options, I realised that they are the basis of the same strategies that we can use when we are under attack, when we are picked on, and when we are being bullied. I have put the five strategies into useful tactics that children (and adults) can use.

I call them the BUZ Gimme 5—Bully-proofing Tactics ©

Chapter Twenty-Two

The BUZ Gimme 5—
Bully-Proofing Tactics ©

Walk, Talk, Bounce, Get Help, Bully Shields.

These useful strategies are not presented in any particular order of priority.

Walk

This is an effective way to help ignore the bullying. If you aren't there, they can't pick on you. Walking away is a useful strategy when being picked on, but it is not a helpful strategy in a conflict between friends.

The walk tactics:

o   *Give a quick eye contact.* This is to let them know you heard what they said, but that you are OK and not going to let it bother you.

I remember a workshop with parents where a mother said, 'I get it. I do "the look" when my daughter says something disrespectful to me'. She didn't get it at all. The quick eye contact is nothing more than a quick acknowledgement before walking away, not a glare.

- *Keep your head up.* This to show you are strong.
- *Walk away the 'cool' way.* Use a straight walk with no unnecessary body language.
- Don't say anything to the person. Just choose to ignore them.
- *Say something to yourself to build yourself up.* Like, 'I'm OK. I'm not going to let that bother me.'

The idea behind walking away is to take your power with you. You may be upset about what they have said, but don't show it to them, as this only serves to give them power.

When kids come to talk to me after they have been bullied, I say that they have probably tried the walk strategy already, but with some practice, they could do it better. I often role play some different ways to walk away.

The first time, I hang my head and cry as I kind of run away.

They say, 'That's not a good way'.

I say to them, 'Who has the power?'

'The one who did the bullying'.

'Who gave it to them?'

'You did!'

Then, I walk away in an agro way. I stomp off and mutter some angry words, sometimes threatening the other person.

They say, 'That's not a good way either.'

I say to them, 'Who has the power this time?'

'The one who did the bullying still has.'

'Who gave it to them?'

'You did!'

Often the person who is bullying feels more powerful with the bigger reaction.

Joshua, a ten-year-old, confided in me that some bigger boys were picking on him on the way home from school. When I asked what they were saying, he wasn't specific. He said that they were just threatening. I asked him how he handled it. He said that he walked on the other side of the road. I asked if that was working for him. He said that it was a bit, but that he still felt scared. I asked him to show me how he walked. He didn't know what I meant at first. I asked him to demonstrate what his body looked like as he walked on the other side of the road. He stood up, slouched his shoulders, and lowered his head. I asked him what message that was giving to the other boys.

He said, 'That I'm weak'.

I asked him if that is the message he wanted to give those boys.

He said, 'No.'

I then suggested this to him, 'On the way home from school today, I want you to walk on the same side of the road as them and keep your head up.'

He replied, 'I don't think so, they will probably beat me up.'

I asked him if the boys had ever said, they would do that.

He said, 'No.'

I knew the other boys and knew that they wouldn't do that. He agreed to give it a try.

I saw him a few days later. He seemed somewhat more upright than usual.

I asked him how it went.

He said, 'I did what you said.'

'And?' I probed.

'Well, they said hello to me!'

I then do it the BUZ Tactic way. I give a quick eye contact and walk away the cool way.

'That's good.'

I ask them, 'How did you feel when I walked away like that?'

They usually say, 'I didn't know what to do. You surprised me.'

'Who has the power?'

'You have kept it yourself.'

'Spot on!'

The key to *walk*: *If you are not there, they can't pick on you.*

Talk

It is often very useful and important to stand up for yourself by speaking to the other person in a *firm* but friendly way.

The tactics:

- *Say how you feel* (use 'I messages'. 'I feel . . . ')
- *Say why you feel* that way ('Because . . . ')
- *Say what you want* ('I want you to stop, or I want you to be respectful.')

I made a BUZ card to help children remember these three things. I chose a picture to put on the card. The picture is of a little man lying on an rubber tube in a pool, wearing sunglasses. He looks a bit like a marshmallow. One child, when I was asking if he remembered the three things on the card said, 'You mean the Marshmallow Man card.'

'Yes.' The name has now stuck. Now, I teach kids the Marshmallow Man skills.

When you have to speak to someone who is not treating you with respect:

- **Say how you feel.**
- **Say why you feel that way.**
- **Say what you want.**

I always ask children who come to me for help if they have talked to the other person about it. They usually say, 'Yes.'

I ask, 'What did you say to them?'

They usually say something like, 'Can you please stop being mean?'

I say, 'That's nice. Did it work?'

They say, 'Not really.'

I respond by saying, 'Sadly, being nice doesn't always work in this situation, that's why you need to be *firm*. Next time, tell them how you feel, why you feel that way, and what you want. (The Marshmallow Man). Don't say please.'

I tell them that the word please, for some reason, makes it sound weak. This is one occasion when saying please will not always be helpful. Be firm, but friendly.

I often do some role plays with the child so they get some practice. I get the child to pretend that I am them. I tell them to tease me, and I will talk to them. I ask them to tell me which way works the best. Here are some of the things I say:

In a weak way, I say, 'You hurt my feelings. Can you please stop teasing me?'

'No!' They shake their head.

'If you don't stop teasing me, I'm dobbing.'

'No!' They shake their head.

'How would you like it if I called you names?'

'No!' They shake their head.

'Stop it. I don't like it!'

'No!' They shake their head stronger.

'You're being mean to me. Stop it.'

'No!' They shake their head.

Finally, I look them in the eye and say, 'I feel upset when you call me . . . , I want you to stop.'

I say it in a way that is quite convincing, in fact so convincing that they think I am being serious.

'Yes, that's it!' They say convincingly. It's like a light bulb has lit up in their head. It makes sense to speak to someone like this when they are not treating us with respect.

Sometimes, older children say, 'Isn't that a bit heavy or serious?'

I say, 'Yes. If you want someone to stop picking on you, you need to be serious. You need to look them in the eye and tell them.'

There is the power in the Marshmallow Man.

There are two other tactics that can be added to *talk*.

- o *Ask the other person*, 'Have I done anything to make you treat me this way?' Or 'Are you angry with me for some reason?'
- o *Be prepared to say 'sorry' if you have done something wrong.* This can be a pretty sure way to get them to stop treating you with disrespect. Maybe they have been treating you badly because they think you have done something to them. This is often a sure way to find out if it is a conflict. If so, you have already taken the first steps on the Hopscotch.

The key to *talk*: *Be firm but friendly with your words*

Bounce

Bounce back a retort.

This is another opportunity to say something to the person who is picking on you. It only works when they are saying disrespectful things and it only works if you are good at it. It requires quick, clear, and often abstract or clever thinking. Usually, children under seven haven't acquired the skills to do this well yet. Bounce backs are about balancing the power or taking the power out of the bullying.

Bounce backs don't always work. They can sometimes be a bit risky, especially if you do them in front of the person's friends or if you tend to be giving more of a putdown than a bounce back.

The tactics:

- o *Say something funny back*—humour has an uncanny way of taking power out of a situation. I get children to role play and call me baldy. My bounce backs include, 'I'm not bald. I'm just too tall for my hair.'
- o *Surprise the other person with a compliment*—it's less easy to pick on someone who is being nice to you.

At a parent workshop I was conducting, Ellen, an eleven-year-old girl who was attending with her mother, put up her hand and asked if she could say something. I said that it would be great if she did. The parents were all ears. Ellen said that when she was new to her school, she noticed a small group of popular girls in the class. Her first impression was that she liked them. One day, the girls picked up her bag and wouldn't give it back to her.

'When they asked me what I was going to do about it, I said, "Nothing, because I like you girls." They put my bag down and left me alone.'

o *Invite them to do something with or for you*—sometimes, what appears to be one child picking on another, by saying something mean, is actually a clumsy attempt to make friends. If you invite the person who is picking on you to be a friend, then often they may stop picking on you.

I remember when I was a boy, a girl used to poke me all of the time. One day, I asked her why she kept poking me. She said, 'Because I like you.'

Andrew, a year one boy, was referred to me because another boy kept hurting him and being rough with him. When Andrew came to see me, I asked if it would be OK to get the other boy and talk to him about it. He agreed. Before we got the other boy, we practiced what he was going to say to the boy. 'Say how you feel, say why you feel that way, say what you want.'

Andrew practiced, 'I feel upset and sad when you hurt me and keep being rough. I want you to treat me better.'

When the other boy came, Andrew looked at the other boy in the eye and spoke well. The other boy dropped his bottom lip and replied, 'I just want to be your friend'.

It's moments like these that make me say, 'I love my job.'

There were no further hurting incidences between the boys. I did find out about three months later that Andrew had been going through grief around the time before the meeting. His separated father started going out with a new girlfriend. It had a devastating effect on Andrew, and at the time, he lost his 'social confidence'.

- o *Agree with them (without putting yourself down).* They don't really have anywhere to go with this, at least for a while. If you are not bothered by what they say to you, it no longer gives them power.
- o *Deflect*—this is about saying things that deflect the power of their words. It includes saying things like, 'You're entitled to your opinion'; 'Sorry, what is that you said?'; 'That's what I thought you said'; 'Do you feel better now?' The key to deflecting is to show the other person that their words of insult will just not stick.

In my office, amongst a myriad of other props and things, I have two pictures. One of a duck and one of a sponge (actually—SpongeBob). I often ask children when teaching them this tactic, 'What's the difference between a sponge and a duck?'

Once they get where I am going with this, they say, 'A sponge soaks up the water and the water runs off a ducks back'.

'Which one are you when people tease you?'

They get it! And the feel empowered by it.

I came across a good website with a great YouTube clip on comebacks. It is called *pockit rockit*. Cofounder Lucy Thomas shares comebacks (not insults) for dealing with bullying.

I prefer to use the word 'Bounce-back' rather than 'comeback'. Comeback sounds a little vindictive or vengeful.

Lucy says, 'Just because you are treated like a loser, it doesn't mean you are one.'

The key to *bounce*: *Be clever, but friendly with your words.*

Get Help

This is a tricky tactic. As children get older, they tend to believe that getting help is not an option, because they believe it may only make things worse. I believe this has a lot to do with us as adults and how we have handled children asking for help when they were younger. When children are younger, they are often told not to 'dob'. What tends to happen when children dob is one of two things. They are either told to go away and don't dob or the adult responds by going to the other person and telling them off. There are, however, some clever adults who know some useful processes that help children to work through the issue with them.

Getting help is about getting support, so that you feel stronger, to balance the power. It is not about getting someone to solve the problem for you, it is about getting the resources to be strong enough to deal with it yourself. Sometimes an adult may need to intervene if the bullying has gotten out of hand. The most effective way of an adult intervening is to use the Restorative Justice process as described earlier in the book.

Here is an example of a situation where Jacinta, an eleven-year-old girl, came to me for help. She said that an older boy in her class was teasing her, calling her names, and putting her down in front of his friends, who joined in the teasing.

The boy was one of the student councillors at the school.

After talking with her about the options, she said that she had tried them but the teasing had continued. I asked her how she felt about having a meeting with the boy so that she could talk with him directly, with my support. She was reluctant, but agreed after I explained that I wouldn't take sides but I would just give her a chance to tell him how she felt.

We invited the boy to join us. He looked nervous and embarrassed as we walked across the playground to my office. I said to him that he wasn't in trouble, just that Jacinta wanted to talk to him about something that was bothering her.

We sat down on the comfy couches in my office. I asked her to tell the boy how she felt, why she felt that way, and what she wanted. (Marshmallow Man)

She told the boy that she felt hurt and sad because he had been calling her hurtful names in front of his friends. He immediately dropped his head in shame, looked remorseful and apologetic.

What made it more powerful was when Jacinta said, 'What hurt the most was that I like and respect you and I didn't think you would treat me like that.'

The boy almost immediately apologised. He said, 'I was teasing you so that my friends wouldn't tease me. I actually like you, but I didn't want my friends to know that, otherwise they would tease me.'

He went on to say, 'I will stop, but please don't ask me to tell my friends to stop.'

The girl agreed. 'I just mostly wanted you to stop'.

I checked a week later. All of the boys had stopped teasing her as well.

I tell children to get help when they need it, even though it is best if they are able to handle the situation themselves.

There are times when getting help is necessary. Find someone you trust, someone who will listen and support you. Not someone who is going to tell the other person off or punish them. Tell them what happened, how you feel about what happened, and what you have done so far. If you need their help actually, ask them for it.

Say, 'Can you please help me with something?'

The key to *get help*: *Getting help is a sign of strength, not weakness.*

Bully Shields

Bully shields are really about your self confidence or your social confidence.

When I teach children the Gimme 5 strategies on a one-to-one basis, I get to the bully shields. I tell them that this is probably the most important. Your bully shields have a lot to do with how you feel about yourself and what is happening in your life. When there are sad things in your life or when something bad has happened at home, it is like your shields have a crack in them or they are down.

When I explain this to children, I ask, 'Is there anything happening in your life at the moment that might be making a hole in your shields?'

I am absolutely blown away nearly every time. The child begins to cry or tries very hard to hold back the tears as they tell me about something that is happening at home or with family. The kinds of things vary from, family breakdown, grandma being very sick, dad being away, mum and dad fighting, not getting along with stepdad, pets dying, and basically anything that a child is grieving.

When I ask them, 'Have you talked to anyone else about this, or does anyone else know how you feel?' Nearly every time, the answer is 'No. Who else is there to tell?'

I am so taken by the courage and honesty of these children as they explain their predicament. I get them to talk about their feelings and help them find the strengths to help them through this time and help them re-power their shields.

Hence, *All power to the shields.* When children regain their confidence, they are empowered to handle things so much better.

I sometimes ask children to name a child in their class that never gets picked on or bullied by anyone. Unsurprisingly, they usually mention a child that I am thinking of. I ask them why they think that the child doesn't get picked on. Some of the answers I get include:

'Because they are nice.'

'Because they are friendly to others.'

'Because they are good at things or confident.'

'Because they are often smiling and don't get angry much.'

'Because they treat others with respect.'

'Because they are positive.'

The list of attributes that children mention fit into the five elements to making a Build-Up Zone or Bully shield.

(Ways to strengthen yours and other's bully shields or regain your social confidence)

- o *Build up your confidence*
- o *Have a group of supportive friends*
- o *Handle your feelings*
- o *Change negatives to positives*
- o *Treat others as you want them to treat you*

The BUZ Gimme 5 Bully-proofing tactics do work, no matter what age you are. They are very powerful. They may not all work all of the time.

One tactic on its own may not be enough. The more you use the better. You will have to decide which ones to use and when you need them.

Sometimes things may seem to get worse for a while. For the tactics to work, the person who is doing the bullying will lose power over you. They won't necessarily like this at first and may try harder for a while. Stick to your guns. Don't stop doing these tactics. Some children have come to me after trying one or two of them only once and have said that they don't work. That's like going to two piano lessons and saying, 'I can't play the piano!' That's right. It does take practice.

When I talk with adults about bully-proofing themselves, I don't vary from these same principles. I may change the language slightly.

The key to *bully shields: build yourself up*.

Chapter Twenty-Three

The Golden Rule and Self-bullying

Ultimately what stands here is the golden rule. *Treat others the way you want to be treated.*

There are two parts to this rule. One is how we treat others. And the other is how we want to be treated ourselves. Unfortunately, some people don't believe they should be treated respectfully. How can we expect others to treat us with respect if we don't have self-respect?

Sometimes the person who bullies us the most is ourselves. Think of the times you have put yourself down, underestimated your abilities, didn't believe in yourself, and called yourself names. Maybe when someone else has not respected us, we believed we somehow deserved it. All these things serve to pierce holes in our shields, reduce our power, and erode our social confidence.

It is my observation that people who get bullied a lot seem to have a low self-esteem. While I agree that any sustained bullying is sure to drain anyone's self-esteem, on many occasions, part of the reason that people with low self-esteem get targeted is because their shields are weak or down. People who are wishing to usurp their power will first of all look for a weakness, vulnerability. Therefore, one of the strongest defences against bullying is to empower the shields. Get your self-confidence back.

I remember asking a bubbly, happy, confident six-year-old girl, the kind that teachers love to have in their classes, the kind of child who might get a book award at the end of the year for citizenship, if ever she gets picked on or bullied.

She said, 'No, not really.'

When I asked her why, she said,

'Because I know who I am.'

I was gobsmacked. Here was a child who summed up the whole concept of bully-proofing in one swift wave of the tongue. She was socially confident.

Social confidence is about knowing who you are.

I asked an eccentric, humorous, happy, and confident twelve-year-old boy if he ever gets picked on.

He said with tongue in cheek, 'All the time, Steve.'

'Does that bother you?' I asked.

'No, because I am strong!'

His shield is firm.

> When people are cruel, it makes all the difference, to know where you're going and where you come from.
>
> (Stephen Fischbacher)

I was impressed with the movie *Invictus,* where Nelson Mandela becomes the President of the Republic of South Africa. For nearly thirty years, he suffered the indignity of imprisonment. During that time, he remembered who he was and where he came from. His bully shield was intact. One of the things that strengthened his shields was his ability to forgive those who imprisoned him in the first place. The rest is history.

After performing our 'Gimme 5—Bully-proofing' show at a school, a boy came up to us and said, 'I really liked your show. It made me feel good. I feel like nothing could ever hurt me.'

We were so taken by his feedback; I asked if we could use his quote. He said, 'Yes.'

On our next visit to the school to do another BUZ show, the same boy came up to us. This time he spoke to us before the show. 'Do you remember me? I am the boy who said the quote. The quote boy.'

We said that we remembered him well.

He went on to say, 'Remember there were two boys who used to bully me? Well, they don't anymore. I used the *walk* method that you taught us in your show. So, every time they tried to pick on me, I just walked away. They must have got bored with no one to pick on anymore, so they left the school.'

We received an email from a mother. 'My son has had trouble with a boy at school for all of term one. I asked him why he was not doing anything about it. So we got his BUZ Gimme 5 pack out and did a couple of role plays. He went to school confident and after one week the boy now waits for him out the front of the school with other boys—not to pick on him—but to hang out with him. Also, the boy has started to come over after school. I am very proud of my son and so is he of himself. Your work is making positive changes out there; you just don't get to hear all of them.'

'All power to the shields.'

Chapter Twenty-Four

The Odd Chapter

I wasn't sure where to place this odd chapter in the book. I didn't put it earlier, because I didn't want this to become the focus of the book. It didn't seem to fit with the flow of the middle section of the book. So, I plonked it here.

Bullying at Home

Unfortunately, the majority of bullying can often happen in a child's home.

Whenever I conduct programs in schools or on camps and we discuss bullying or bully-proofing, I often ask questions of the children around the subject. By far, the most examples children give of examples of people picking on them are about their brothers and sisters. When I put the question, most children I speak to say they get bullied more at home than school.

A Potpourri of Stories

I remember my little sister scratching the back of her heel once, and for some reason, at least one of my brothers and I took advantage of the situation. We teased and tormented her for days with the chant, 'Scratched the back of your heel, you heel!' Or something sinister like that. What was that about?

My little brother told me that my elder brothers and I used to pin him down and hang some spittle from our mouths and then suck it back up.

Sometimes it would drop. How cruel was that? I'm so ashamed that I used to do things like that. Sorry, little bro.

I remember a woman telling me that she feared her father. She said that he was a powerful man, and she felt intimidated by him. She went on to say that it wasn't bullying, because she believed that he didn't intend to hurt her.

Sometimes the people who are meant to love us the most are the ones who treat us the worst. It might not be classed as bullying per say, but it could be abuse. I'm pretty sure every parent who abuses their child would say that they didn't intent to hurt their child.

In my experience working with children, I have listened directly to many children's accounts of abuse; physical, verbal, psychological, sexual, emotional, neglect, and withholding of love. I have seen the devastating effects to their psychological and emotional well-being. For many children, the depletion of their social confidence finds its roots in the child's home.

Without a doubt, one of the most devastating events in any child's life is the breakdown of the family unit. Children are often disempowered in the whole process, before, during, and after the actual breakdown. While parents experiencing marital breakdown don't actually set out to hurt their children; unfortunately, they are tremendously hurt as a by-product of the breakdown.

The reality could be that the worst bullying happens in a child's home in the forms of abuse, neglect, and withholding of love, where they are meant to feel the safest.

Parents should rightfully have a degree of control over their children and their behaviour. This implies a certain degree of power.

If bullying is about a power imbalance, at what point does a parent cross the line from parental guidance to that of bullying control where the power is out of kilter?

I believe it is down to one word, 'Respect'. Children should be treated as a treasured heritage not a possession.

This next story is quite bizarre.

I was once approached by some parents from a school to run a program to bully-proof a whole year level of children. They were concerned that their children may end up in a certain teacher's class in the next year. The parents believed that the teacher bullied the children and didn't respect them. In their mind, they thought if the children could learn some bully-proofing skills before they go into the teacher's class, they would be able to survive the year.

I asked if they were serious. They said, 'Yes.'

I did tell them that this sounded more serious an issue than any program could fix. My advice was that they have a discussion with the principal of the school about their concerns. They said that they had, but not a lot could be done.

I don't wish to elaborate on systems that tolerate the ill-treatment of children in this book. We do live in a world where children need responsible adults with the courage to stand up for their rights and protection. There was a time when children had little rights. We still have a long way to go.

When our state and social systems bully children, collectively we have a responsibility to bring about the necessary social change. These systems include the media, institutions that care for children, the advertising machine, and commercial ventures that take advantage of and exploit children.

One other area that we as a society are only just coming to grips with its impact on and exploitation of children is the whole cyber world, including the Internet and social networking. Governments and policy makers seem to be playing catch-up with appropriate controls and, dare I say, 'censorship' to protect children.

Chapter Twenty-Five

Cyber Bullying and Social Networking

The acts of 'wrong relationships' as described by Izzy Kalman have spilled over onto the social networking world of our younger generation.

Over the last five or more years, I have noticed not just an increasing number of issues related to relationships between children on the Internet but a lowering in the age of children that have access to all the forms of social media. When Facebook first started, it was designed for uni-aged. In time, the age for joining was lowered to sixteen and sometime later lowered to thirteen. I know of children as young as six with FB accounts.

I recently asked a six-year-old what she got for her birthday. She said, 'An iPad.' She is now on FB.

I don't wish to expand on this whole world of children and cyber issues to any great extent in this book. It can be an incredibly emotive issue. I'll leave it to the media machine to continue to run with that.

Unfortunately, the social networking and cyber bullying is often not viewed in the whole context of relationships, conflict, and lack of respect. There is a lot of misleading information and a tsunami of inflammatory stories on cyber bullying. Sometimes there is so much focus on cyber bullying by the media, school departments, and parents that little attention is paid to general relationships skills.

Cyber Bullying and Teenage Suicide

A very common yet unfortunate theme is the link between teenage suicide and cyber bullying. Unfortunately, the acts of bullying cop the full brunt of blame in many cases of teen suicide. I am not denying that the bullying happens and that sometimes the bullying contributes to a young person feeling so bad that he or she makes that tragic fatal choice.

Young people who attempt suicide have much deeper issues than just being bullied. Most of the time it is those deeper issues that have diminished their social confidence, which makes them more vulnerable to bullying.

There is much being done about youth depression and the prevention of mental health issues in young people. Unfortunately, much of what is called 'prevention' is more so 'intervention'. This intervention is extremely important and should be valued. It is my opinion that our prevention of depression and mental health doesn't kick in early enough. Much of our government and corporate funding is aimed towards the bottom of the cliff. Some is aimed at putting up fences at the edge of the cliff. Not enough is getting to the top of the cliff itself, building up children from a much younger age with the social and emotion skills to live life safely on the top without venturing near the cliff. You can read more about this in the book *BUZology*.

Whatever we can do to build young people up should be championed, so that they have enough value in themselves, where they have no thoughts of taking their own lives.

How to Be Cyber Savvy

In the whole cyber bullying process, I would like to concentrate on two areas. The first being conflict, and the second being bullying, which is a form of conflict with a power imbalance.

Some of the major apparent bullying issues between children on the social sites have actually arisen from unresolved conflict in day-to-day relationship that spills over into social networking sites. This is mostly between girls, but not always.

Let me take you back to an email I received many years ago. A particular person was not happy with me because of something I didn't do that she was expecting me to do. Instead of talking to me about it face-to-face, she decided to email me. The email was quite scathing of me. I was upset by the things that the person was saying to me that I knew weren't true. Even though it was a once off, I felt bullied. I felt disempowered because I didn't have a chance to defend myself of the accusations before they were put in writing. I remember thinking that the person didn't have the courage to speak with me face-to-face about the issue.

I replied to her email by saying, 'Can we meet to discuss this?' We did sort it out in time. However, I did come away from the experience with a conscious decision never to sort out a relationship issue or conflict via email, because of the effect this experience had on me. I believe that face-to-face is the most effective and most respectful way to resolve conflict.

It's interesting that Facebook is called what it is; actually, if you think about it, it's really is 'Facelessbook'. Part of the reason why people use social media to pick on, show disrespect, and bully people is because it is faceless. Many children have told me that the reason others bully online is because they are gutless to say it to the other person's *face*.

There is a saying that goes like this, 'Any words spoken in anger are words that may be regretted later.' The same could be said for any words written in anger.

Things that Go Bump in Pre-Teen Relationships

A ten-year-old girl, Cassie, showed me a conversation she had with a friend via 'Bump', an iPad app, that allows you to message another person who has 'bumped' their iPad with yours. Cassie was trying to say to me that the other girl had written some bad things about her.

Cassie was most upset because her friend, who didn't really want to have the conversation, typed the word, 'OKAY' about twenty times in a row. She got upset with the responses, so she said something mean and regretful. The mother of the other child saw what Cassie had written and that she was getting angry, so she took over from her daughter and typed the words, 'Can we talk about this when you have calmed down?'

We'll, Cassie was livid at this as she told me, 'How dare she tell me to calm down!'

When I looked through the conversation she had on her iPad, I pointed out to Cassie all of the angry words and mean words she had typed and that her friend had not typed anything that was offensive but just wanted to talk it out with her but not over 'Bump'.

She realised that she may not have handled it well and agreed when I asked if we should get the other girl and talk about it together. The girls did a good job expressing their feelings. The other girl explained to Cassie that it was her mother who wrote the words, 'Calm down.'

They told me that the whole thing started when the two girls decided to take some videos of themselves dancing in some 'compromising' positions and removing their outer clothing. (Remember, these girls were ten!) Doing this together created a myriad of emotions between the girls, and they both blamed each other and felt embarrassed, ashamed, and guilty. They also told me that they did feel a kind of excitement when they were doing it even though they knew that it was a bad thing to do.

The whole world of social media, Internet, personal tablets, PCs, mobile phones, digital cameras, and cyber world is like a Pandora's Box for children. Most children are sensible, aware, and savvy enough to keep themselves safe. One of the girls in the previous story had a positive relationship with her mother that allowed her to tell her mum (almost) everything that happened.

What I have come across is a fairly large degree of self-regulation amongst children in the cyber world. The reality is, in time, that they will relate the same values system in the cyber world as they do in the real world. Sometimes I have seen a greater sense of sticking up for someone or speaking out when something is not right amongst children online. However, I have seen a particular nasty and vindictive side as well.

As a parent or carer of children, you can decide on the level of monitoring that you place on your children. They need to know that you are there for them, are approachable, not critical in a closing or negative way, but ready to offer support and a solid 'moral' base.

There are plenty of websites that give great advice for parents about supporting and monitoring their children in the cyber sea.

Chapter Twenty-Six

Social Networking Hints

- Don't use social sites to sort out fights with others. It can often make it worse. It is best to do this face-to-face; it is much more respectful.
- If someone continues or starts a fight with you online, you could say to them, 'Can we meet to talk about this?'
- Once it's posted, it may be difficult to remove—so think carefully before posting anything.
- Would I like someone saying this to me?—A question to ask yourself before posting a comment.
- Keep your user name and password to yourself (don't even share with your best friend).
- Keep private—private—be careful about what you share online.
- If you don't feel comfortable about something, it could be a good sign that it is not safe or right.
- If you are not feeling right or safe about something, talk to an adult you trust.
- Be respectful of other people's content in the same way you would like people to respect your content.
- Remember—once the 'ENTER' button is pressed, it's almost impossible to stop it. So don't press it if you are really angry or upset with someone.

Chapter Twenty-Seven

Online Bully-Proofing Tactics

The same tactics for bully-proofing can be used for online or cyber bullying. They just need a different slant or interpretation.

Walk (ignore)

Switch off, block, delete, de-friend.

Anyone who is on social media knows what these mean and knows how powerful they can be. If someone's messages are blocked, you can't see what they are saying about you. The problem with this is that a number of young people actually want to see the bad things people say about them. I'm not sure why this is the case. It possibly gives them more reason to not like the other person. They can sometimes feed off the negativity if they have any self-doubt, it will just be reinforced. There is a choice for young people here. Switch off, ignore, or leave on.

Talk (communicate)

Write back in a sensible and controlled way. Let the other person know that you didn't appreciate what they said. If it is a conflict with a friend, you could say, 'Can we meet to talk about this?'

You could also use words similar to the Marshmallow Man. Say how you feel, say why you feel that way, and say want you want. For example, I felt hurt, when you posted . . . , I want you to be more respectful, or stop.

This is not as effective online as it is face-to-face. Emoticons can come in quite useful here. If someone says something to you or about you that you don't like, you can send them a sad face.

Bounce (retorts)

Retorts can be useful. Bounce back something to them as a response to any message or post. Remember the basic rule for good bounce backs, 'Be clever, but friendly with your words.'

Get Help (support)

Get support from friends, online and offline, and advice from trustworthy adults, parents, and teachers. Report any abusive or inappropriate posts to the administrators of the social networking site. There are good checks in place and heaps of advice online. Google it!

Bully Shields (personal power)

Keep your confidence up. If there are difficult things going on in your life, get the support you need from friends or family or other people you trust, people who will help build you up. If you have some self-doubt or personal issues that are affecting your self-esteem, there is a good chance that you will be more vulnerable. Remember the five elements to make a Bully Shield apply.

1. Build up your confidence
2. Have a group of supportive friends
3. Handle your feelings
4. Change negatives to positives
5. Treat others as you want them to treat you

Chapter Twenty-Eight

Final Words

Caught in the Crowd

A few years back, a great song was released on the market called, 'Caught In The Crowd', by Kate Miller-Heidke. It's a song about a boy she met at school whom she got to know. They shared stories about how their families had broken up and they became friends. One day, the boy was being bullied by a group of boys who knocked him around a bit and said that he had no friends. He said that he did and looked up at her, but she just walked away. Looking back on the experience, she wanted to say, 'Sorry'. She wanted to say that she was just part of the crowd.

A Better Version of Themselves

Many years ago, I was working in a school as a volunteer pastoral care worker. I got to know many children including a group of year six boys. One of the boys was very much like a Mafia boss. I liked him. He was cool, calm, and collected. He had a group of friends, but he was definitely the sophisticated Alpha male. His friends followed him around and looked up to him. They had a bit of a reputation of being the 'cool' guys, sometimes not treating others with respect and often putting other kids down who were not part of the group.

One of his best mate's father committed suicide. Both of the boys came and talked with me on a few occasions about it. It was a tough time for the boys. Over time, healing took place. Sometime later, out of the blue, Vince, (I'll call him that as he was an Italian and as I mentioned earlier, he reminded me of a Mafia boss) came to see me.

He said, 'I would like to come and see you with all of my friends and Jamie and his friends.'

Jamie was boy that he and his friends picked on quite a bit. I agreed, wondering what was about to go down. I was intrigued and nervous.

What happened at that meeting was cemented into my memory and opened my eyes to what children are open to and capable of.

The boys all gathered into a room with me. Vince got all of his friends to sit down. Jamie and his friends sat down. I looked at Vince and said, 'Well, Vince, it's over to you.'

Vince looked up at Jamie and in front of all of his friends said something like this, 'Jamie, I just want to say sorry for the way I have always treated you. It hasn't been fair of me to pick on you and bully you.'

This was huge. I mean, huge! In front of his friends. He was taking a big risk. He was genuine. Something happened to make him want to take this step. It wasn't provoked or encouraged by anyone. He did it off his own back, his own volition. His friends didn't know about it. The other boy didn't know about it. It took courage and integrity.

He looked Jamie straight in the eye as he spoke the words with honesty and integrity. I looked at Jamie as he began crying. Now, this wasn't a weak cry. It was the cry of a boy, actually, a young man, who for some time had lived under a fear of being treated badly and been bullied by others. The tears were tears of hope and relief from pain. It came as a sheer surprise to Jamie.

As Jamie cried, Vince said, 'I'm really sorry! I don't want to treat you that way ever again.'

Jamie accepted his apology. The rest of the boys hardly said a word. They didn't know where to look. Vince's friends were caught up in the whole business of teasing Jamie and now they were being challenged to look at themselves and their own motives.

A new respect for Vince grew in Jamie and his friends, in me, and in Vince's friends. This was one of the most powerful things I had ever seen. I had the privilege of being there.

Vince had been bullying Jamie and he had got his friends to do some of his dirty work. Vince wasn't a bad kid, far from it. Somehow, something brought Vince to this point. It might have been the challenges of having a friend lose his dad. Somehow, this boy looked at himself and decided to make a better version of himself. That day, the world became a better place.

Many years later, on an entirely unrelated occasion, I received a Christmas thank you card from a parent. It said the words, 'Thank you for helping make my daughter a better version of herself.' I shed a tear. I saw a connection. This was one of the best snippets of feedback I have ever received.

Every child has the same capability to be a better version of them-selves. Will we give them the chance? Will we allow them the freedom?

In the dedication of this book I referred to Meoke. After I heard the tragic news of the unnecessary death of Skye, an amazing 15 year old girl, I woke up in the middle of the night with the word *Meoke* in my head. The next morning I Googled the word to see if there was any meaning or connection. I came across a fascinating short story of hope and freedom, hence the reference. If you are interested, you will find the story at this web address: *http://www.bucconeer.worldcon.org/ contest/05ff_h06.htm*

Meoke will be free

Chapter Twenty-Nine

In Summary

o Bullying happens.

o Bullying is not normal. It is antisocial.

o Most bullying comes from unresolved conflict.

o Much bullying happens between children who used to be friends.

o Punishing 'bullies' often only serves to make it worse.

o It is a false expectation that punishment helps children learn right from wrong.

o To eliminate bullying, we need to create communities of respect, connectedness, positivity, and restorative practice. (The excellent way)

o More Respect = Less Bullying

o There is no such thing as a 'bully', but people can do bullying things.

o Bullying is about power imbalance.

o Bully-proofing is about balancing the power.

o Validating a child's feelings is a great first step to support them when they have been treated disrespectfully.

o One of the most effective inoculations against bullying is the skill of conflict resolution.

o The BUZ Gimme 5 Tactics for Bully-proofing©: Walk, Talk, Bounce, Get Help, Bully Shields.

o The Marshmallow Man rules.

o Getting help is a sign of strength not weakness.

o Cyber bullying is an extension of lack of respect in relationships.

o The same tactics for bully-proofing can be used for online or cyber bullying.

o Young people who attempt suicide have much deeper issues than just being bullied.

o Children are often bullied in their own homes.

o Without a doubt, one of the most devastating events in any child's life is the breakdown of the family unit. It has the terrible effect of diminishing a child's social confidence.

o Grief has a powerful way of reducing children's social confidence.

o Children should be treated as a treasured heritage not a possession.

o Treat others the way you want to be treated.

o Everyone has the right to feel safe and deserves to be treated with respect.

Chapter Thirty

Some Great Children's Picture and Storybooks on bully-proofing skills

When I look for good children's books on bully-proofing, I try to find ones that don't use the actual word 'bully' in them, referring to one person or a group of people as bullies. I usually find these books patronizing for children and not empowering. I look for books that reinforce one or more of the BUZ Gimme 5 Tactics in creative, clever, and empowering ways.

The Magpie Who Wasn't a Chicken—Steve Heron
(Nurture Works)

My attempt to write a story about handling bullying that includes each of the five strategies.

This is the first children's book I have written. It started because a boy asked me to write a story about a boy who gets picked on in the toilets. I told him that I don't write children's stories but I will give it a try. No matter what I tried it just didn't work, until one day I saw some magpies playing on a road near where I lived. It looked like the magpies were playing 'chicken'. A couple of magpies appeared to be forcing another magpie onto to road as I approached in my car. It only takes a spark to get a fire going. This incident lead to a brushfire of children's books. I wrote ten stories in six months and had six of them published.

One—Kathryn Otoshi
(KO Kids Books)

This is one of the cleverest books on bully-proofing I have seen. It is simply created with coloured paint dots and numbers. It explores the important issues of standing up to people who try to overpower you and not just being a bystander.

The Recess Queen—Alexis O'Neill and Laura Hulisha-Beith
(Scholastic Press New York)

I love reading this book to kids. It is a real laugh, but incredibly powerful as Katie Sue, the most unlikely child stands up to Mean Jean the recess queen in a surprising way. I love the made up words in this story, like 'lollapalloosh'.

King of the Playground—Phyllis Reynolds Naylor
(Aladdin Paperbacks)

Kevin discovers the power of self-confidence, guided by a very sensible father who helps Kevin regain his self-confidence. This story has some great 'bounce back' ideas that Kevin gets to use when he is threatened by Sammy. The story starts, 'Kevin puts on his Spiderman T shirt, his batman underpants and his jeans with a horseshoe on each pocket, but he doesn't feel brave and he doesn't feel lucky.'

Some great DVDs/movies

Lilo & Stitch

Lilo & Stitch is a 2002 American animated science fiction/family film produced by Walt Disney Feature Animation.

I am a big fan of some of the animated children's movies. The producers do their research with children and pretty much get it right. No more than in one of my favourite movies, *Lilo & Stitch*. If you haven't seen it, go to the video store, get it out, even if you don't have kids. I know it has been around for ages, but is still popular with children from four to nine. It can now be classed, in my opinion, as one of the classics.

In the movie, Lilo is somewhat a social outcast. She doesn't have friends. She gets picked on by Myrtle, the bossy girl. Lilo retaliates on one occasion by bopping myrtle on the nose with a punch. Lilo adopts a dog (well, actually a creature from another planet—Stitch). I think she is attracted to it because it reminds her of herself. He is aggressive, obnoxious, and lonely.

They become companions. In one scene, after some mayhem caused by Stitch being out of control, Lilo draws a picture of Stitch and colours him in red up to halfway up his head. She says to him, 'This is your badness level. We're gonna have to fix that.' How does she fix it? By teaching Stitch about 'Ohana'. Ohana means family, family means no one is left out or forgotten. Both Lilo and her sister Nani have some anger issues and have experienced severe grief as they lost their parents in a car accident.

The movie touches on all of the themes of social confidence, conflict, bullying, anger and feelings management, family, grief, and respect. I love this movie; it falls in line with all of my experience, research, and thinking about these issues.

Steve Heron

The Mighty—Miramax films

I've cried in quite a few movies, but this one takes the cake. It is a story of two boys who have an unlikely friendship. One boy is crippled with a terrible disease. He lives with his mum. His dad cleared out when he was born. The other boy is a giant of a fellow, being brought up by his grandparents. Dad is in prison. Both boys encounter bullying and together they make a formidable force as they bully-proof themselves.

It is a powerful movie that has references to King Arthur, the Knights of the Round Table and nobility.

Unfortunately, it receives an 'M' rating; as one scene is considered violent or it could be the couple of swear words that appear in the movie. Recommended viewing for 10-to-100-year olds.

The Mighty is a 1998 comedy-drama film directed by Peter Chelsom and based on the book *Freak the Mighty* by Rodman Philbrick.

Bibliography

Best Friends, Worst Enemies, Michael Thompson, Catherine O'Neill Grace, and Lawrence J. Cohen, Ballantine Books, New York 2001.

Bullies to Buddies: How to Turn Your Enemies to Friends, Izzy Kalman, Wisdom Pages, Staten Island, NY 2005.

Bully is a 2011 documentary film about bullying in US schools. Directed by Lee Hirsch, the film follows the lives of five students who face bullying on a daily basis, Weinstein Company.

The Bully: The Bullied and the Bystander, Barbara Coloroso, Quill-Harper Resources, New York 2003, 2008.

The Friendship Factor, Kenneth H. Rubin, Ph.D., professor of human development and director of the Centre for Children, Relationships, and Culture at the University of Maryland and Andrea Thompson, a freelance writer based in New York City, Penguin, New York 2002.

The Optimistic Child, Martin Seligman, Random House, New York 1995.

Real Justice: How We Can Revolutionize Our Response to Wrongdoing, Ted Wachtel, The Piper's Press, Pipersville, PA 1997.

Something Fischy CD, Stephen Fischbacher, Fischy Music, Edinburgh.

www.restorativejustice.org.au/leading/oconnel Terry O'Connell, Order of Australia Medal, Director Real Justice Australia.

Other books by the Author

BUZology—Powering Hope in Children
Steve Heron
Published by Nurture Works © 2011
www.buildupzone.com/shop

BUZ Feel Safe Feel Right Series—Children's books

Picked Last
A story about loneliness and making friends
"The crabs at the estuary have a favourite game. Crab Soccer!"
Gerry is a lonely crab who discovers some keys to making friends

ISBN 970 0 9803692 0 5

The Magpie Who Wasn't a Chicken
A story about handling bullying
"Hey, are you a chicken or what?"
Nick uses his courage to get away from a sticky situation.

ISBN 978 0 9803692 3 6

The Ging
A story about the strong feelings associated with physical abuse
Zing! The rock flew from the ging.
Andrew's anger fizzed inside of him always wanting to burst.

ISBN 978 0 9803692 1 2

Skimming Stones
A story about overcoming a family breakdown.
Often Gary would go for a walk along the river and skim stones
across the water. He wanted more than any thing else in the
world for his parents to get back together.

ISBN 978 0 9803692 5 0

A Terrible Secret
A story about courage to disclose sexual abuse
"Can I trust you with a secret?" Asked the girl.
A girl finds courage to tell someone what has happened to her.

ISBN 978 0 9803692 2 9

The Land on the Other Side of the Rainbow
A story about death, sadness, grief and hope.
Whenever Melissa saw a rainbow, it would bring a smile to her
face as she remembered her Grandma and the pelican who
showed her the rainbow on that sad morning.

ISBN 978 0 9803692 4 3

www.buildupzone.com/shop

CPSIA information can be obtained at www.ICGtesting.com
Printed in the USA
LVOW08s1741290114

371502LV00001B/268/P